Positive Placements

A companion website to accompany this book is available online at:
http://education.midwinter.continuumbooks.com

Please visit the link and register with us to receive your password ar
access these downloadable resources.

If you experience any problems accessing the resources, ple
contact Continuum at: info@continuumbooks.com

Also available from Continuum

Positive Placements
Making the Most of Your Educational Placement

David Midwinter and
Tracy Whatmore

continuum

Continuum International Publishing Group

The Tower Building   80 Maiden Lane
11 York Road   Suite 704
London SE1 7NX   New York NY 10038

www.continuumbooks.com

British Library Cataloguing-in-Publication Data
A catalogue record for this book is available from the British Library.

ISBN: 978-1-4411-9542-5 (paperback)
        978-1-4411-4952-7 (hardcover)

Library of Congress Cataloging-in-Publication Data
Midwinter, David & Whatmore, T
Positive placements : making the most of your educational placement/
David Midwinter and Tracy Whatmore.
    p. cm.
Includes bibliographical references and index.
ISBN 978-1-4411-9542-5
1. Student teaching–Great Britain. I. Whatmore, Tracy. II. Title.

LB2157.G7M53 2011
370.71'141–dc22

                                                    2010043983

Mixed Sources
Product group from well-managed
forests and other controlled sources
www.fsc.org Cert no. TT-COC-002769
© 1996 Forest Stewardship Council

Typeset by Newgen Imaging Systems Pvt Ltd, Chennai, India
Printed and bound in Great Britain

Contents

Acknowledgements

We would like to especially thank Carolyn Allen, Rachel Dovey, David Meechan, Sally Roddy and Adelle Ronson. They shared wonderful presentations about their placements that thrilled their audience, and inspired us to produce this book. We hope that you will capture some of that excitement as you read extracts from their case studies.

We would also like to thank the following students who permitted us to use their writing in case study extracts: Jennifer Adkins, Jassbinder Heyer, Gemma Nicol, Naomi Sambrook, Johanna Smith, Adam Swarbrick and Stephanie Zeal.

There are many students, teachers, university tutors and friends we have worked with over numerous years who have contributed to our experiences and have indirectly influenced the advice and guidance we offer in this book. Thank you all.

With special thanks to Alison (at Continuum), Ruth, Sarah, Simon, Tony, Shirley, Ron, John, John and Pam for their invaluable support, feedback and suggestions.

Introduction

The initial idea for this book came from the amazing accounts that students gave after undertaking placements, in a diverse range of educational settings. A national conference was organized so that student representatives, from a number of Higher Education Institutions, could present their accounts to a wider audience. The conference was a resounding success and the presentations were inspirational. A report of the event with video footage was put on the ESCalate ITE website (www.escalate.ac.uk/ite). Further details are available on the website that accompanies this book.

The presentations included information about appropriate preparation for the placements and provided vivid details of the experiences gained. The students also articulated the powerful impact of these experiences on their academic, professional and personal development. It was immediately apparent that the students had gained such a huge amount from these placements that their experiences should be shared with a much wider audience and that these experiences could encourage and motivate others. Thus the decision to produce an accessible and 'reality' based text to support and guide students and teachers in preparing for and undertaking placements in national and international educational based settings.

The book has been produced for students who are considering, preparing for or undertaking a placement in an educational setting. Whatever you are, a student on an undergraduate degree or a postgraduate programme, we hope you will find plenty of useful advice and guidance. The focus of the text will especially support student teachers intending to work in schools or educational settings. However, students on non-teaching programmes that involve a placement in an educational setting will also find lots of information that will be useful in preparing for and undertaking a placement.

All student teachers spend a significant part of their training undertaking placements. The majority of these placements will be in schools or nurseries, and we will refer to these as 'traditional' placements. However, since 2002 training providers have been encouraged to allow students to have placements in 'non-school settings' and the number of these placements has grown considerably. We shall refer to these placements as 'alternative' placements. These are often a highlight for students, partly because there is more individual choice and flexibility in alternative placements and as such there is focused advice and practical strategies for alternative placements, in each chapter of the book. There are also increasing opportunities for students to participate in 'international' placements, and we provide comprehensive guidance that will be useful if you are undertaking, or considering undertaking, a placement in an educational setting abroad.

The book is divided into nine chapters, which focus on key aspects of preparation for and undertaking, a placement in an educational setting. Each chapter follows a set structure, to make each as accessible as possible. This includes: a summary of the chapter outlining the key areas to be considered; subheadings to highlight the focus of each section; lists, scenarios and examples to illustrate points being made, and provide practical guidance; case study extracts to provide 'real life' accounts from diverse placements; questions to consider after each case study extract; and key points to aid future reflection and action.

Throughout the book much is made of case study extracts, written by students during and after their placements. We want you to be able to benefit from the experience of other students and be inspired to have positive placements of your own. We hope that you will be encouraged by their accounts and stimulated by their enthusiasm, motivation and obvious enjoyment of working with children and students in a diverse range of placements. It is apparent in all the case study extracts that the students prepared thoroughly, put in a huge amount of hard work and carefully reflected on what they had learned and experiences they had gained. Hopefully you will learn from them, and from the advice and guidance that is offered. Further case studies can be found on the website that accompanies this book.

Part I
Before You Go

Why Go on Placement?

Summary

Placements should be the most exciting part of training to be a teacher, and the highlight of programmes that include educational placements. It is hugely rewarding when you see that children and students are learning new knowledge, understanding and skills from the work you are doing with them. As such, placements can provide opportunities that could be life enhancing and even life changing.

The title of this chapter might appear to be a very straightforward question; but there are many answers depending on who is answering the question. There are various people who have a role to play in every placement. Understanding the expectations and concerns of all those involved will help you get the most out of the placements that you undertake.

We will explore how those involved in placements will have different expectations, perspectives and issues, depending on what role they have. We will consider traditional school placements and see how the head teacher will have different expectations and views from the mentor, the class teacher and the children and students. We will examine Special Schools, and how their context changes the expectations and issues for those involved. International placements and alternative placements will be discussed and we will demonstrate how the answers to the question, 'Why go on placement?' can be many and varied. Understanding the expectations and potential anxieties of the people involved in providing your placement will help you prepare for a positive and enjoyable experience.

Traditional school

If you are training to be a teacher in England, you can expect that most of your placements will be in a 'traditional' school, which are generally state funded and provide free education for children and young adults between 4–18 years of age.

Case Study: Sally – Traditional

Sally wrote about her expectations and initial concerns after her first visit to a school where she was about to undertake a 4-week placement in a year five class:

> Before commencing the placement I was a little apprehensive and wondered what value the placement would be, given that I had already developed a strong preference for teaching within Key Stage 1. For logistical reasons the children were grouped in ability groups by the school. It became clear that the children knew their 'rank' within the class in terms of academic achievement and ability. I quickly realized that overcoming the perceptions the children already held of themselves as learners and of their ability to achieve was going to be a significant challenge.
>
> Another challenge I identified was the need to resist the temptation to 'teach to the test'. The school was under pressure to improve its annual Standard Assessment Task (SATs) results and it was evident that the staff felt this pressure. I also observed the impact that this pressure had on the staff and their teaching styles and general approach to learning when mixed with the hectic demands of day-to-day life in school. In my experience it made many of the staff, inadvertently in most cases, narrow the curriculum and 'teach to the test'. This was a philosophy that I had always strongly disagreed with and yet I did not want to be responsible for the children not achieving the desired results.

Consider:

- How could Sally have prepared for the change from Key Stage 1 to Key Stage 2?
- What strategies have you seen employed in school, or read about, to ensure breadth and balance is occurring in an overcrowded curriculum?

Sally highlighted some of her own anxieties, and understandably, they related to her desire to do well on the placement. She also demonstrated sensitivity to a potential clash of agendas concerning teaching styles and SATs. Being able to identify the potential for a difference between your hopes and expectations and those of your placement school is very important. You should always remember that on a placement, you are an invited guest, and that the invitation can be withdrawn, just as it was offered.

Case Study: David – Foundation Unit

David was placed in the Foundation Stage Unit of a Primary school for his final placement. The Unit included all of the nursery and reception aged children, and a number of key adults.

The Unit had three class teachers and three teaching assistants, some of whom job shared throughout the week. There was also an autistic child who received full time one to one support when at school. During the six weeks at school I was responsible for registering the twenty children in 'blue group'.

The school was in a predominantly white middle class suburb and had been labelled as an 'outstanding school' during its last OFSTED inspection. Previously the Foundation Setting had consisted of two Reception classes and a Nursery, but had been made into an integrated Foundation Stage Unit. I was at the school during the second half of the autumn term.

My initial thoughts were those of apprehension, as I was joining a team that worked very well together with a clear understanding and expectations of one another. I would need to find my own role and place within this already established team. This was made more difficult, as at face value I could not distinguish between class teachers and teaching assistants. Everybody seemed to do as much as the next person, from leading activities to tidying up and making the tea. What was at first frustrating for me to try to decipher, was actually what made the team and Unit so successful.

The other potential challenge was that I would be entering an all female team. However this would not be a new situation, as having worked part-time in Early Years settings, this was something I had come to expect. The initial surprise and excitement I was usually greeted with, when arriving at a setting, then gave way to a minefield of role identity within the setting. What could be deemed as stereotypical, I spent most of the first week outside, gardening and building. I therefore consciously made an effort to spend an equal amount of time inside and outside during the following weeks. Going into a female dominated teaching profession is always going to prove very educational for both my colleagues and myself. After the first two weeks, however, I felt part of the team. Admittedly, I didn't know exactly what part, but a part.

Case Study—Cont'd

Consider:

- Are there particular skills that you have that will help you to develop a role within the setting you will be working in – such as playing an instrument, being artistic, being able to speak different languages?
- What do you think some of the challenges might be when you begin your placement? How can you prepare for these?

David highlighted two initial concerns. First, he found it a challenge to understand the exact roles of each person in the Unit. This made it difficult for him to see how he would fit into the setting. Understandably, this created some initial anxiety, but he soon found a role. His second anxiety concerned gender. Educational settings and schools, especially in the Early Years and Primary age phase, tend to have significantly more female teachers, and few, if any male teachers. By this stage in his course, David was accustomed to this situation. So he ensured that he developed his own role within the setting, and managed to extend his involvement beyond improving the outdoor environment.

Head teacher

Generally speaking, head teachers in schools are keen to help participate in training teachers of the future, which is why they offer student placements. They have a vested interest in teacher training and preparation, because it is very likely that at some point in the future they will need to appoint new teachers, and they want them to be as effective as possible. They also recognize that it is very good professional development for teachers to work with students. It is often not until you have to explain something to someone else that you realize how much you know and understand. Supporting a student is also a positive way for the teachers to gain new and different ideas. If a student is going to be working with the children and students for a substantial amount of the time, head teachers recognize opportunities for the teacher to develop other work during that time, as well as being available to support the student, if needed.

One of the concerns for head teachers (HTs) when they agree to take a student on placement is that it may be time-consuming for the staff involved, and could be perceived as a significant amount of additional work, as well as a benefit. You should be aware of this, and try to ensure that you avoid taking up more of the teacher's time than is really needed.

Mentor

Most schools will have a designated teacher who is responsible for students. They may have a different title, depending on where you are studying, but their role is to mentor you on placement, to give you constructive feedback and advice. If you are a student teacher your mentor will also need to assess your progress against TDA (2008) Standards for Qualified Teacher Status (QTS). Mentors are teachers who have a strong desire to help students become effective teachers and they have often received specific training in how to support, guide and assess students.

Although mentors are willing to help you in all aspects of your placement, they have expectations of you. They want you to be enthusiastic and eager to learn. They will not expect you to know everything, but they will expect that you are committed to the placement, and willing to work hard and be as well prepared as you can be. However, they will expect you to be interested, listen to and act upon advice. Although this may sound fairly easy to accomplish, you may find that in fact it can be quite challenging as you might not always agree with your mentor. It is fine to have a professional conversation with your mentor, but remember that they have had years of experience and if, after discussion, there is still a disagreement you need to follow your mentor's advice.

Two of the most significant initial concerns for a mentor, are that a student will not listen to or act on advice given; or not be fully committed to the placement and not give the time and effort that is expected. Teaching and work with children and students can be very demanding, and teachers often work many hours in addition to the time they are actually in a school or setting. This may lead to mentors sometimes finding it frustrating, when they consider that sufficient effort is not being put into the placement or that advice is being ignored and issues are developing.

Class teacher

In some situations your mentor and class teacher will be the same person; but in other situations they are not, and it will be the class teacher you will spend the most time with. Although many of the teacher's hopes for and expectations of the placement will be similar to that of the mentor, the class teacher will have some that are particular. During your placements you will become increasingly aware that the children and students become very important to their teachers, and hopefully to you. Teachers will care very deeply that the children and students do well. As a result, they will want you to demonstrate that you can be effective before they feel confident to give you increased responsibility for the class.

The children's and student's learning is paramount and class teachers are bound to have slight apprehension that their learning might be effected if a student takes on some of the responsibilities. However, as long as you are willing to work hard and act upon advice, you can dispel those initial concerns and develop positive relationships with teachers, staff and the children and students in the setting.

Special schools

DfES (2004) 'Removing Barriers to Achievement' set out the Government's vision for giving children with special needs and disabilities the opportunity to succeed. This document stated that all children should have opportunities to learn, play and develop alongside each other, within their local community of schools, with shared responsibility and a partnership approach to their support. Children with special educational needs tend to be included in mainstream schools whenever appropriate and possible. Nevertheless, there are many Special Schools, which can provide enlightening and valuable placement opportunities for students and teachers. There are different kinds of Special school and they may have specific areas of need that they cater for, such as:

- Generic special needs schools
- Dyslexia specialist and dyslexia friendly schools
- Schools for children with speech, language and communication difficulties
- Autism and ASD (autism spectrum disorders) specialist schools
- Schools for children with sensory impairments, physical and medical needs
- Schools that specialize in emotional and behavioural difficulties
- Schools for children with global learning difficulties: MLD schools, SLD schools and schools for children with profound and multiple difficulties and complex needs
- Special Units that are attached to mainstream schools.

Some of the most obvious distinctions between Special Schools and mainstream schools are that the number of children and students in a class tend to be fewer; and that the number of adults involved in the education and care of the children and students will tend to be higher. Generally, the hopes, expectations and concerns that apply to placements in mainstream schools are also applicable to Special Schools; although there may be some significant differences, as highlighted by Sally.

Case Study: Sally – Special school

Sally outlined her thoughts after a first visit to a Special school for a placement:

> On entering the setting I was struck by a number of concerns. I was shocked by the severity of some of the children's needs and was particularly apprehensive about how I was to facilitate learning for children who could not, for a variety of reasons, access the curriculum as every child I had taught previously had. I was very apprehensive that the four week placement would not be long enough to learn all of the new teaching skills that I needed in order to ensure that the students were benefiting from my sessions.
>
> During my visit days I was given information on each child within the Unit. After reading this it became clear that a number of students could exhibit very challenging behaviours and that these behaviours could often be so distracting or disturbing that their peers responded with similar undesirable behaviours on scales I had not previously witnessed. Clearly managing behaviour was going to be a significant challenge on this placement. Another challenge that I identified was going to be addressing the massive variation in attainment levels between the pupils in the class.

Consider:

- How could Sally find further information about the specific needs, disabilities, conditions and so on, for the children in the class?
- From observations, reading and research can you identify behaviour management strategies that might be useful when undertaking a placement in a Special school?

Not surprisingly, Sally's greatest concern was behaviour management and how she would cope. Equally, the head teacher and other teachers would have the same concerns regarding how well a student would cope with the behaviour challenges. If you have a placement in a Special school, observe the staff closely and take on board their advice and guidance. They are used to working as a team, and it will be your aim to become an effective member of the team.

The second area of concern to Sally was how to make the learning appropriate because of the wide range of special needs that prevented the children from accessing the whole curriculum. Even within a Unit of 11 children there was a huge range of ability. The hopes, expectations and concerns of all parties are very different in a Special school, and it is important to consider this before opting for a Special school placement. This will be considered in more detail in Chapter 2.

International placements

Many Higher Education Institutions (HEIs) offer wonderful opportunities for undergraduate (UG) students to undertake 'international' placements, abroad. If you are a postgraduate (PG) student you may have the opportunity to be involved in an international placement, if you are focusing on Modern Foreign Languages (MFL), for example. These provide the chance to gain experience of preparation for, and participating in, learning and teaching in an international context. Placements abroad can enable you to critically analyse practical and pedagogical issues encountered in learning and teaching in an international context; to extend knowledge, understanding and skills in relation to learning and teaching; to gain experience of international settings and the wider context of educational provision; and to investigate the structure and organization of learning and teaching in international contexts.

'International' placements can be undertaken in various countries, as part of organized programmes, or arranged specially by your training provider or you. There are funded placements which are organized as part of an internationally recognized programme. The Erasmus programme, which is European Union (EU) funded, facilitates the opportunity to study abroad for a minimum of 3 months. Usually, within this time there will be the opportunity to undertake a placement in an educational setting.

Erasmus is the European Commission's flagship educational programme for Higher Education students, teachers and institutions. It was introduced with the aim of increasing student mobility within Europe. Erasmus forms part of the EU Lifelong Learning Programme (2007–2013). It encourages student and staff mobility for work and study, and promotes transnational cooperation projects among universities across Europe. The scheme currently involves nine out of every ten European higher education establishments and supports cooperation between the universities of 31 countries. Erasmus has developed beyond an educational programme – it has acquired the status of a social and cultural phenomenon. It gives many European university students their first chance to live and thrive abroad. Well over 1.5 million students have benefited from Erasmus grants to date, and the European Commission hopes to reach a total of 3 million by 2012 (www.britishcouncil.org/erasmus).

Another part of the EU lifelong learning initiative is the Leonardo programme. 'The Leonardo programme supports the development of skills and training. It funds work placements for trainees, workers and staff, and supports European projects to discuss common issues or develop training materials, courses and frameworks' (www.leonardo.org.uk/). It enables students to be funded for teaching placements abroad. These are organized by the training provider where you are studying. To be part of this project, they will need to have European partners who will provide the placements. If you are studying modern foreign languages (MFL) as a specialist subject, a placement abroad may be a mandatory part of your course. Your training provider will organize this, but as with other placements the more you can find out about the placement, the more confident you will feel.

There are a wide range of non-funded opportunities to do placements abroad. Some of these placements may be organized by your training provider, while others you may be able to organize for yourself, although your provider will need to know exactly what you are arranging. International placements tend be undertaken in schools, however some may be in other types of educational setting such as nurseries, Children's Centres or Special schools.

If an international placement is a mandatory part of your course it will probably be assessed, but some international placements are not assessed, so hopes, expectations and concerns may be different.

Case Study: Adelle – America

Adelle was looking forward to an international placement in America.

> When given the school details my initial instinct was to 'Google' them, and then when looking at the statistics and information many thoughts and questions popped into my head. Would the Hispanic community speak English as a first language or Spanish? Would the children be aware of where I came from, all the way across the Atlantic Ocean? Also, how economically deprived were the children? These questions and thoughts would only to be answered when we got there and met the children in person. One major challenge that was identified was how much did the children know about the wider world and was this with an American perspective on their thoughts and ideas.

Consider:

- How would you find out about the country, location and setting for your placement?
- How would you try to ensure that your pre-conceived ideas did not have a negative impact on your preparation, or the placement itself?

The concerns expressed by Adelle are typical of what most students feel when planning for an international placement. It is an opportunity to meet new people and experience living in a new culture. It is a chance to travel and enjoy new sights and new food, but it is also challenging not really knowing what the placement will be like. In this country the placement expectations of all involved are carefully managed by your training provider; but it is much more difficult for providers to manage what happens when you are abroad. Therefore, your expectations need to be different. For example, when the placement has been organized by your training provider you can assume that the school or setting where you are doing your placement will have a good idea of what to expect. However, in an international setting staff may be unlikely to have the same detailed understanding of your course and previous experience. This will be especially true if the educational system; structure, content, curriculum, training and so on, are different from those in England.

When the placement has been organized by you and the school or setting has had no previous experience of working with your training provider they may have little idea of what you will be hoping to do, and may have diverse expectations of you. The staff at the placement may imagine that you know a lot more about their educational beliefs and practices than you actually do, or underestimate what you can and should be doing.

When accepting students from abroad, the school or setting may well expect you to be confident and enthusiastic, and perhaps more independent than you actually are. They may assume that you have initiative, new ideas and are flexible. Hopefully, you will have all of these qualities, but it may be useful and perhaps necessary to clarify that although you have undertaken some training, you still have a lot to learn, and that the experience will be different from any other you have had, so you may need a little time to adjust.

You need to be prepared for any eventualities, because the situation may be so dissimilar from others you have experienced. Available resources may be far fewer, or far more, than you are used to, and they may be different. You may be expected to teach larger or smaller size classes than you are used to or, in some situations, you may not be able to teach as much as, or more than, you anticipated. Whatever the expectations are, you will need to be as adaptable as possible and to try to meet them. It may sound daunting, but this is part of the excitement of international placements; and as long as you are prepared for the unexpected and are willing to keep an open mind and work hard, you will have a memorable experience.

Case Study: David – Japan

David outlined his international placement, in Japan:

The bulk of my placement in Japan was to be in a local, government run elementary school. Children begin elementary school when they are six years old and progress through grades one to six before entering junior high. There were three classes in each year group, comprising of between thirty and forty children. Each classroom physically mirrored the next and there were no classroom assistants. The school also had two special needs classes which were separated into physical and mental disability, but these often joined together for activities and lessons. The special needs classes were small and of mixed age ranges but children would return to their year group for particular lessons and activities.

I was also fortunate to be invited to several other educational institutions. I visited one nursery school, two kindergartens, two elementary schools, two junior high schools and one senior high school. I attended university lectures at undergraduate and postgraduate level. All university lectures were in English and when visiting other institutions there was always someone who could translate, so questions could be asked by both the visiting and visited. It is worth noting that nursery schools are seen as less academic and serve those mothers who wish to return to work early, whereas kindergartens are more academic with children beginning at a slightly older age. The experience of visiting such a variety of institutions gave me a very brief overview of the system as a whole. I was able to see the different stages that a child/teenager progresses through and the development of different pedagogical approaches throughout the system.

The placement was to be a minimum of twenty days but we were given the whole of the spring term to complete it. This meant I spent just over three months in Japan. For the duration of the time, my own aim was to absorb as much culture and language as possible, as this was needed for me to fully benefit from the placement itself. The initial language barrier was a concern, but I often had translators on hand to assist with any questions and answers. Indeed, the language barrier highlighted many alternative means of communication that are often available, but often overlooked and underutilised.

My initial reactions were of excitement at the opportunity to experience another education system. This opportunity, at such an early stage in my teaching career would also have great benefits for my professional development; especially when applying for jobs eighteen months later. I knew the experience would also make me step outside of a culture and education system that I had been part of all my life. I recognized that through doing this placement there would be both rewards and challenges. My major concern was about communication as I spoke very little Japanese and the majority of the Japanese people I would meet spoke very little English.

Consider:

- If you decide to undertake an international placement in a non-English speaking country or location, how could you prepare for this?
- Are there resources that you could utilize, or develop, that might aid effective communication in the placement?

Like many other students who choose to do an international placement David was confident and enthusiastic. He was eager to gain as much as possible from the opportunities available to him. Communication was his greatest concern at the start of the placement, but he did not allow this to deter him from gaining as much as possible from his placement.

Alternative placements

Due to the limited amount of time on a PG programme, extended alternative placements, which last for a few weeks, are often not possible. However, some PG programmes include 'special' or 'focus' weeks when groups of students go into alternative settings or schools, en masse and engage in theme weeks or something similar. These provide a wonderful opportunity to be more adventurous in your teaching, and to witness learning and teaching in different contexts. Alternative placements have become a feature of many undergraduate (UG) programmes.

Circular DFES 02/02 introduced the 'Qualifying to Teach Standards' (QTS) and for the first time teaching in non-school settings was encouraged. The requirements for Initial Teacher Training (ITT), issued in conjunction with Qualifying to Teach, stated 'R2.5: Teaching in settings other than schools may also count towards these totals (number of required weeks in school) provided they enable trainee teachers to work towards the achievement of the Standards'. This was further encouraged by the Teacher Development Agency (TDA) in 2007.

The TDA fully supports the Teaching Outside the Classroom initiative which should provide trainees with the opportunities to gain an understanding of working with the creative and other sectors and give them the skills to bring creativity into their own teaching, hopefully utilizing this throughout their teaching careers. The QTS Standards fully allow, and indeed encourage the use of alternative settings as a means for trainees to meet those standards.

In 2008 the Teaching Outside the Classroom programme was launched by Creative Partnerships in partnership with CapeUK, the Museums Libraries and Archives Council (MLA), the DCSF Learning Outside the Classroom Manifesto (LOtC) and the Training and Development Agency for Schools (TDA). The following is an extract from the press release that was issued at the launch of this programme:

> 'Jim Knight, Schools Minister, said:
> Every child can benefit from direct learning in exciting environments such as theatres, museums, galleries, outdoor education centres and sports clubs. These

opportunities are increasingly important in nurturing the creative skills of young people, as laid out in the Learning Outside the Classroom Manifesto. This programme will help give new teachers the skills and experience to deliver those opportunities. I hope all providers of teacher training and settings across England are able to use these resources to work in partnership.

The Teaching Outside the Classroom programme is a key opportunity to influence the next generation of teachers, collaborate with a diverse range of providers and settings, and help put creativity and partnership working at the heart of Initial Teacher Training' (DCSF Press Release 4 March 2008).

'Jacquie Nunn, Director of ITT Development at the Training and Development Agency for Schools, added:

The TDA fully supports the Teaching Outside the Classroom programme. This programme should provide trainees with the opportunities to gain an understanding of working with a range of contexts including the creative and cultural sectors and give them the skills to bring creativity into their own teaching, hopefullyutilising this throughout their teaching careers. The QTS Standards and requirements launched this year fully allow, and indeed encourage, the use of alternative settings (at venues concerned with the learning of young people) as a means for trainees to meet those Standards' (DCSF Press Release 4 March 2008).

The press release, gives us an insight into the hopes and expectations of the Teaching Outside the Classroom programme. However, the hopes and expectations of the placement settings and of the students may well be different. Unlike schools, these settings are not taking students for the purpose of training the next generation of teachers, but do offer an insight into various organizations which may contribute to your future role.

There are a significant number of diverse, alternative placement possibilities. Normally, the main criterion that is applied is that the placement must enhance your development as a teacher or student, and that gives a huge amount of scope. The following list is indicative of the types of placements that students have undertaken. It is far from an exhaustive list but gives you some idea of the range of possibilities:

- Museums
- Art galleries
- Football clubs
- Outdoor education centres
- Community projects
- Children's hospices
- Wildlife centres
- Libraries
- Zoos

In the next chapter we will look in more detail at how to choose the right placement for you, but first we need to consider what the purpose of undertaking alternative placements is. Prior to 2002 alternative placements for student teachers were rare, but learning outside the classroom can be viewed as very beneficial to children and students; consequently teaching outside the classroom has become more significant.

Carolyn undertook an alternative placement and she outlined her expectations.

Case Study: Carolyn – Art Gallery

I picked an art gallery in the Lake District, for no other reason than it wasn't too far away and I quite like art. I spoke to the Education Officer on the phone who agreed to a meeting and the rest, as they say, is history. The host decided I wasn't too much of a liability and agreed to take me for a three-week placement in the Summer Term. My first visit to the gallery enlightened me to the fact I would be spending three weeks in a beautiful Georgian building, surrounded by stunning paintings and sculptures, with the rolling hills of the Lake District as a backdrop. On top of that, the gallery had a workshop where activities with local school groups took place – local 'middle-class' school groups. This wasn't what you would call a 'socially deprived area'. You couldn't actually fail this placement they said. Apparently they wanted us to just enjoy the experience and learn as much as possible from the setting. I was feeling pretty smug with myself and looking forward to a . . . well . . . a doddle of a placement. Hell on earth would now be heaven on earth for three easy-weeks of arty fun, without the worry of possible failure. Hurrah!

Those were my initial thoughts . . . unsurprisingly they didn't last very long! Yes, this was a different kind of placement but it was still a teaching practice which meant there were still many challenges looming ahead regarding the usual suspects – planning, behaviour management and assessment. The difference in setting didn't matter one bit, these issues would still have to be addressed. On top of this, there was the added challenge of attempting to teach in a non-school setting, with none of the usual school resources and lesson structures that I was familiar with. Questions immediately began to run around my head. What would I be teaching? Would there be proper lessons? How would I teach? What would I teach with? Would I have a classroom?

Consider:

- How might Carolyn begin to address some of her questions and concerns?
- What other challenges might there be if you undertook a placement in an alternative setting?

Carolyn recognized that the challenges of this placement were going to be very different from those faced on a traditional school placement, but relished the opportunity.

Understanding each other's hopes, expectations and goals is crucial to a successful and positive placement, as we have illustrated throughout this chapter. In the next chapter we consider how to choose the right placement for you.

Key points

- Placements are often the most exciting part of a course or training programme, so make the most of the opportunities provided and become immersed in your placements!
- There are many people involved in a placement, and all will have different expectations and concerns which you need to be aware of.
- Traditional, alternative and international placements will bring their own diverse expectations and potential concerns.
- Understanding the expectations and concerns of others, as well as your own, will be a significant factor in the success of your placements.

Resources

www.britishcouncil.org/erasmus
www.leonardo.org.uk/
www.teachingoutsidetheclassroom.com

2

How to Find the Right Placement for You

Summary

Most placements are found for you by your training provider, but now that there are more opportunities for placements in alternative settings and international placements there may be choices to be made. Thus, this chapter will focus on the various potential issues and considerations that need to be taken into account when choosing an alternative placement or an international placement. We will look at the many opportunities that are available and will pose questions to help you decide how to find the right placement for you. For traditional school placements, you may be asked to express preferences and we will consider the options open to you.

Traditional school placement

Although you are usually not allowed to arrange your own placement, you will be asked to express a preference. This will usually be in regard to location, type of school, faith school and Key Stage, so we will consider each of these in turn. The temptation is to request a placement as close to where you live as possible so that you have to travel less, however this should not be the only criteria to use. You may have personal circumstances that affect how far you can travel. If you have a medical condition that limits the distance you can travel, in which case you probably need to obtain medical evidence from your doctor and give this to your placement office.

If you have family commitments, this may also affect how far you can travel. You need to be aware that training providers cannot demand that schools will take students and in some areas of the country the demand for local placements is greater than the supply. In these cases you may have to travel further than you would ideally like. You may have work commitments that mean you would like to be placed near to home, but again it may not be possible to place you near to your home.

As you consider location, you should think about gaining a variety of school experiences. If you have already been placed in an inner-city school you would benefit from a placement in a rural school or a town school if this is possible. You should also consider where you are living while you are on placement. If you live close to your training provider but your home address is also within the training provider's area of work, this might be an option. If you lived at home or with friends or relatives for the duration of your placement, would this open more possibilities in terms of the range of schools available? Some training providers offer placements in other parts of the country, which may be far from where they are situated. It is certainly worth considering these distant placements, as they can be very rewarding and add to your range of experience.

In making a decision about location there are three particularly important points to consider. First, when you apply for your first teaching post, it will be beneficial if you have had a range of experience, including locations. Secondly, contemplate where you want to work when you qualify. If you are able to do a placement in that area it may be useful. Thirdly, remember you are not choosing where you will do your placement, you are only expressing a preference; and such is the demand on school placements in certain parts of the country, you may not be placed where you would ideally like to be.

Another preference you may be able to express, concerns the size of school. If you are hoping to work in a rural area, it might help you to gain experience in a small school. This may sound idyllic but there will still be challenges. For example, you will probably have several age groups in the same class, so planning may be more complicated and time consuming. Working in a two or more form entry school is a challenge at the opposite end of the scale. You will find yourself working with at least one other teacher, and support staff, so that lessons are the same for all classes in the year.

There are also different types of school, as detailed:

The four main types of state school all receive funding from Local Authorities. They generally follow the National Curriculum and are regularly inspected by Ofsted.

Community schools

A community school is run by the Local Authority, which:

- employs the staff;
- owns the land and buildings;
- decides which 'admissions criteria' to use (these are used to allocate places if the school has more applicants than places).

Community schools look to develop strong links with the local community, sometimes offering use of their facilities and providing services like childcare and adult learning classes.

Foundation and trust schools

Foundation schools are run by their own governing body, which employs the staff and sets the admissions criteria. Land and buildings are usually owned by the governing body or a charitable foundation.

A Trust school is a type of Foundation school which forms a charitable trust with an outside partner – for example, a business or educational charity – aiming to raise standards and explore new ways of working. The decision to become a Trust school is taken by the governing body, with parents being able to contribute to this decision.

Voluntary-aided schools

Voluntary-aided schools are mainly religious or 'faith' schools, although anyone can apply for a place. As with Foundation schools, the governing body:

- employs the staff;
- sets the admissions criteria.

School buildings and land are normally owned by a charitable foundation, often a religious organization. The governing body contributes to building and maintenance costs.

Voluntary-controlled schools

Voluntary-controlled schools are similar to voluntary-aided schools, but are run by the Local Authority. As with community schools, the Local Authority:

- employs the school's staff;
- sets the admissions criteria.

School land and buildings are normally owned by a charity, often a religious organization, which also appoints some of the members of the governing body (www.direct.gov.uk).

Academies

It is also important to mention academies, as the present government is keen to promote the creation of many more academies.

Academies are publicly funded independent schools that are intended to provide a first-class education. Academies can benefit from greater freedoms to help teachers innovate and raise standards. These freedoms include:

- freedom from Local Authority control;
- ability to set your own pay and conditions for staff;
- freedom from following the National Curriculum;
- ability to change the lengths of terms and school days.

See www.education.gov.uk/academies/

In practice, many of these schools are very similar to each other. However, if you hope to work in a faith school in the future, it may be helpful to have a placement in a faith school. Most faith schools in England are either Roman Catholic or Anglican, and you can express a preference for a placement in one of these schools. Alternatively, you may prefer not to do a placement in a faith school, and you may express that preference also.

Finally you may need to consider which Key Stage you are going to request, if this is an option on the course you are on. Your first two placements will be in two consecutive Key Stages, as this is a requirement in order to gain Qualified Teacher Status (QTS), but if you have a third, and maybe fourth placement, you may be able to express a preference. If this is the case you will need to consider how much you want to challenge yourself or whether to go for the 'safest' option. If you have had a very successful experience in a year two class, for example, you may want year two again because you enjoyed it and feel confident in your ability. However, you may not have had any experience in some of the other Key Stage Two classes and a placement there might broaden the range of classes you feel confident with. As noted, you will only be expressing preferences, but it may be worth giving these issues some thought.

Alternative placements

How to find the right placement for you is a much more pertinent question with regard to alternative placements. Knowing where to begin can be complex, so consider the following questions:

- Do you want to do something you already know about? For example, if you are interested in sport, you could try to find a placement in an outdoor centre.
- Do you want to try something completely new?

- If you have somewhere in mind, how will that placement help you become a better teacher or develop certain knowledge or skills?
- What do you want to gain from this placement?

Case Study: Carolyn – Art Gallery

After initially observing and examining what the gallery already had in place, I began to see the potential for using my own teaching expertise to adapt some of the existing workshops. I planned my own re-vamped sessions using the same resources in different ways. I gained the permission of the education officer to deliver these re-vamped sessions to visiting school groups. The first session I planned and delivered was called the Portraits session, aimed at a group of Key Stage 1 children.

The main learning objective for the session was to understand how artists reproduce the face in portrait work. The session was based around the visual stimulus of a sculpture and paintings of portraits displayed in the gallery. First the children would look closely at portrait work produced by artists before having a go at sketching and copying some of the facial features they could see in the artists' work.

Soon after the success of adapting and delivering the Portraits session, a local school contacted the gallery enquiring if they had a workshop suitable for their year 2 class, focused on the topic 'People Who Help Us' which they were studying in school. At the time the gallery didn't have any such workshops so I volunteered to do a new session which would be more suitable. Again I focused the session on a visual resource already present in the gallery – a huge landscape painting of Lake Windermere by eighteenth century artist Philippe Jacques De Loutherbourg. The painting is titled 'Windermere in a storm' as it depicts a stormy Lake Windermere with a small boat and it's passengers in trouble. The painting shows some figures reaching out to help the passengers to safety. I entitled the session 'Helping Hands' and prompted a discussion with the children about people who might help in such a situation as depicted in the painting. Afterwards the children went to the workshop area where they could choose from a variety of practical, cross-curricular activities relating to the topic Helping Hands.

Towards the end of the placement, my confidence in using the gallery's resources as a tool for cross-curricular teaching had grown to such an extent that I progressed to designing a whole new workshop for the gallery to use with future school groups. I based the session on a painting called 'The Gower Family' by George Romney. It aimed to combine teaching art and PE dance objectives.

I am pleased to say the workshop was a success; both the children and I thoroughly enjoyed the experience and gained a lot from it. I asked the teachers of the visiting group to complete an evaluation of the session and

Case Study—Cont'd

was happy to read comments saying they were 'very pleased with the whole visit, the workshop was excellent – well prepared and delivered.' They said they felt their pupils benefited from 'the opportunity to visit a gallery, with a high standard of art work and to listen and work with such enthusiastic professionals.' To hear such comments from experienced teachers visiting the gallery was the real highlight of the placement for me.

Consider:

- Even if you do not undertake a placement in an alternative setting such as an art gallery, how could you utilize this facility to support your work with children? For example, could you prepare a pack in preparation for a trip to an art gallery, or could you collect resources from an art gallery that you could use in another setting or school?
- Are there local facilities, historical sites or environmental features that would be suitable for trips for children and students? Could you gain information from these and develop preparation packs?

Carolyn's placement was a great success because she was enthusiastic and determined to get as much out of the placement as she could. She worked with the Education Officer and also used her initiative to grasp every opportunity that was open to her. Whatever placement you decide to do, if you follow Carolyn's example and put in maximum effort you will find it a richly rewarding experience.

In order to help you decide the type of placement you would like to pursue, we will consider a wide range of options and what the benefits of each might be. With each of the options we have included the views of a student about to undertake a placement.

Museum

Museums have an important role in the education of children. Education officers who work for the museums services prepare teaching packs for school visits and make history come alive for children. They are an ideal venue for an alternative placement and offer the opportunity to learn new skills.

My role will be to help out in the museum developing a teaching pack for schools and developing activities for early years children. I will also be observing different teaching strategies such as role-play and object handling. This will give me a different view on teaching. I will be developing my own historical knowledge, and how to use historical sites, (Undergraduate student).

Outdoor adventure centre

If you have an interest in sport then the opportunity to do a placement at an adventure centre seems too good to be true. However, it is important to remember that you will be a member of staff, and much may be expected from you with regard to taking professional responsibility. If you only see this as an opportunity to enjoy yourself doing outdoor activities then you may need to reconsider! Working with children in an outdoor environment is very different from being within a school setting. Health and safety and behaviour management issues are paramount. However, it can be hugely rewarding to see children experiencing the outdoors and learning in new environments.

> I will be working alongside the staff learning how the activities are organised and delivered. I will take on more responsibilities for leading the activities as I feel comfortable. The activities provided are: canoeing, abseiling, ropes course, orienteering, teambuilding games, walking, mountain biking, pond dipping and more. There are science and geography classrooms so that children can plan their scientific investigations, for example, for the pond dipping. I will be helping children outside the classroom and the environment so will see how they behave or respond differently. It will give me an opportunity to see how much effort goes into planning a school trip of this kind, and it will give me a chance to work with children of all ages and abilities over a short period of time (Undergraduate student).

Performing Arts College

Taking the opportunity to do a placement in a secondary school is an option that many students consider. It enables them to get an insight into secondary education, to enhance their subject knowledge and to observe new teaching strategies. It gives useful insight into the transition process from year six to year seven.

> I will be joining year seven pupils during their lessons and exploring what work is expected at this level, and how this differs from work given in year six. This experience will enhance my student teacher education by helping my confidence. It will help me to use my voice more effectively and develop different behaviour strategies. I hope to learn about behaviour management and leadership (Undergraduate student).

Hospital school

There are many children who spend long periods of time in hospital. It is very important that they continue to receive education during this time so many hospitals have their own schools. Teachers in these schools need to be very flexible and be able to plan for mixed ability classes. Individual needs have to be catered for, in very specific ways, and a placement in this type of school will give insight into provision for a variety of special educational needs.

> I will be shadowing the full time teachers in the hospital and then I will take on the role of the teacher. This placement will allow me to gain experience of teaching children in a different environment and to provide suitable differentiation for mixed ability children. It will help me to take practical account of diversity as well as promoting equality and inclusion in my teaching (Undergraduate student).

Wildlife centre

There are many different types of wildlife centre, but all of them have an interest in educating children. Different areas of the curriculum are likely to be considered, but perhaps with a particular focus on subject areas such as science, geography, art and history. If you have an interest in these subjects or you would like to improve your knowledge in these subjects then a placement in a wildlife centre may be for you. One example is the Wildfowl and Wetlands Trust. They work towards conserving wetland areas across the world and protecting endangered animals that live in these areas. They have nine centres across the country and are fully prepared for school visits.

> My role will involve being very hands-on with any opportunity I am presented with, in particular with running school tours, directing educational activities, and being a general ambassador and team member of the WWT. I will have the chance to consider and practise new and exciting teaching styles, which I might never have dared to use in the classroom situation (Undergraduate student).

Children's hospice

This kind of placement is not dissimilar to working in a hospital school. However, a key difference is that the children in a hospice are terminally ill. Before considering such a placement, you need to recognize the reality that these children could die at any time. If you can cope with this reality this could be a hugely rewarding and satisfying placement. Terminally ill children still need stimulating education which can often be a distraction from their suffering. You will also have frequent contact with parents who themselves are struggling to come to terms with their child's illness.

> I will be working closely with the care team, learning how to care for these children. I will also be working with the physiotherapist and the bereavement team. This placement will allow me to develop professionally, by enhancing my own personal knowledge and understanding of disabilities. I will be able to do arts, music, and

play activities with the children. I will also gain valuable knowledge on how to deal with parents and families. This placement will be a benefit to me if I ever work in a special needs school (Undergraduate student).

Zoo

The prospect of doing a teaching placement at a zoo may seem very strange. However, zoos play an important role in educating children about animals and their habitats. Children can witness at first hand the feeding and care of all kinds of animals. They can also learn where animals come from and about endangered species. Most zoos have education centres and actively encourage visits from schools, so there are plenty of opportunities to work with children.

I will have the opportunity to work with children in an out of school setting allowing me to see how they learn differently when not in their normal learning environment. I will be working with a variety of different age children from 4 to 11and therefore will get the chance to try out teaching key stage one and key stage two science, and any other subjects that arise from the stimulus of the zoo. I will be taking on the role as one of the team at the zoo education department and will have the chance to integrate into a working environment. I think this will be beneficial for my work experience in the future (Undergraduate student).

Children's centre

If you are an early years' specialist you may have the opportunity to be placed in a children's centre on one of your traditional placements. However, for other students this will not happen, and a placement in a children's centre will be an interesting experience. It will give you the opportunity to observe at first hand the early stages of a child's education.

I will be working alongside the practitioners at the centre, looking after the children and I hope that will develop my skills in teamwork and collaboration. I will work with the parents in the 'positive parenting' outreach work, and I hope to become more aware of policies and practices (Undergraduate student).

Community centre

There are many different education projects that are based in community centres. The centres are often a base for various educational outreach activities into the local community. This may involve working with children of all ages and also with parents. It is very important to discover what projects are run by the particular centre before you commit yourself to going on placement. The following quote is an example of the activities of one particular community centre:

> My placement is working alongside a project coordinator. He provides activities for children of all ages, in order to keep them off the streets and prevent issues such as antisocial behaviour. My role will be working alongside the staff team in a number of structured sessions, some of which are mother and toddler sessions, after-school clubs, multifaith projects and holiday activity programmes. I will be involved in planning and risk assessing future projects and activities. I will observe how factors such as deprivation and racial discrimination can affect the learning and development of children. I will be tackling these problems with community projects. The multifaith projects are taken into school, so I may have an opportunity to attend and assist the team with the sessions (Undergraduate student).

Steiner school

There are many Steiner schools across the country. They are independent schools and their philosophy is based on the ideas of Rudolf Steiner. This is a summary of their ethos, taken from the Steiner website:

> The priority of the Steiner ethos is to provide an unhurried and creative learning environment where children can find the joy in learning and experience the richness of childhood rather than early specialisation or academic hot-housing. The curriculum itself is a flexible set of pedagogical guidelines, founded on Steiner's principles that take account of the whole child. It gives equal attention to the physical, emotional, intellectual, cultural and spiritual needs of each pupil and is designed to work in harmony with the different phases of the child's development. The core subjects of the curriculum are taught in thematic blocks and all lessons include a balance of artistic, practical and intellectual content. Whole class, mixed ability teaching is the norm. www.steinerwaldorf.org.uk/

A placement in a Steiner school will give you an insight into a different style of education and how children learn in this environment.

> The role I will be undertaking will be of support to the teacher, observing the way that the curriculum works and supporting individual children or groups of children. I believe this placement will allow me to concentrate on being more creative in my approaches to teaching. This is something I believe to be important in any school or class, and it is of particular importance in the Steiner curriculum (Undergraduate student).

We have considered 10 different placement options, but there are many more so you have lots of options if you plan in advance. You will find further case studies on the Teaching Outside the Classroom website: www.teachingoutsidetheclassroom.com and on the companion website to this book.

International placements

There may be opportunities to undertake an international placement, as outlined in Chapter 1, but you need to decide whether an international placement is right for you. It is certainly true that an international placement will take you out of your 'comfort zone'. You could be a long way from home, family and friends, and you may need to do quite a lot of independent travelling. It may be that few people speak English in the country or location of your placement; and you may need to be able to cope with the challenges of communication, different food, different money and a different culture. For some people, these challenges will sound daunting and, if this is the case, then an international placement may not be for you. For others this may seem tremendously exciting and an option that is definitely worth exploring.

You may participate in an international placement through the Erasmus and Leonardo programmes, which will be organized through your training provider. Alternatively, you may decide to do a placement that you have organized yourself. If you have friends, relatives or contacts in another country that can help in finding a suitable placement, this could open up all kinds of possibilities.

Stephanie wrote this about her upcoming international placement.

Case Study: Stephanie – Cayman Islands

I will be undertaking my placement in the primary section of a prep and high school in the Cayman Islands, having involvement with children from kindergarten to year six. The School has a strong Christian ethos and boasts a multicultural student body taught by teachers of various nationalities. The school offers a broad and balanced curriculum based on the National Curriculum of England and Wales and also satisfying the education requirements of the US, Canada and the Caribbean. This will give me the opportunity to experience a different way of teaching the National Curriculum and gain an insight into differences and similarities between ours and other countries' guidelines for education.

Case Study—Cont'd

The school affords a range of excellent facilities to enhance the children's learning across an array of core and foundation subjects. Facilities include: numeracy and literacy learning centres, state-of-the-art computer lab with wireless connection to computers in every classroom, custom-designed library, a spacious art/science/DT room, large music room with smaller instrumental practice rooms, a multipurpose hall, and an astroturf playing field.

The role that I will be undertaking on this placement is simply to get involved in all aspects of life at the school. I will be observing and helping out in a variety of lessons, developing professional relationships with staff and students, discovering the history and culture of the Cayman Islands, learning about their cross curricular approach, along with the different learning styles adopted, and upholding the school rules and Christian values. Although I will not be teaching lessons myself, I will be actively involved in the children's learning, especially in my specialist subject, physical education.

During curriculum and extracurricular time, the students participate in many sports, both English and American, from all six areas of the PE National Curriculum. Some of these activities such as American football, softball and sailing are not often incorporated into British PE lessons hence this placement is providing me with a fantastic opportunity to broaden my knowledge, understanding, and experience of a range of different sports, which I can then go on to teach in the UK.

Participating in an alternative placement in an overseas country will enhance my teacher training, because it will give me a once in a lifetime teaching experience in a completely different environment to one that I am used to. Having the opportunity to work in a multicultural school with children of varying social backgrounds will really help me expand my awareness and comprehension of how a range of factors/influences can affect children's learning within an array of contexts.

While I'm on placement, I hope to immerse myself in school life, building professional, cooperative relationships with staff, so I can become a part of a committed, diverse teaching team. With the school curriculum, being based on the English one, but incorporating Canadian, American and Caribbean requirements. It will give me the opportunity to gain awareness of different frameworks, policies and practices. The School has a cross curricular approach to learning, so I will hopefully have the opportunity to increase my knowledge and understanding of a range of teaching strategies. I plan to be actively involved in the children's learning, showing respect for the supportive relationships and demonstrating the expected values and attitudes and behaviours.

Overall, I think participating in an alternative summer placement in the Cayman Islands will give me a valuable experience unlike any other and I cannot wait to experience what teaching in the Cayman Islands has to offer!

Stephanie's case study highlights many of the benefits in undertaking an international placement. If you are considering undertaking an international placement it may be useful to think about the following questions in the light of Stephanie's case study:

- What do you hope to gain from an international placement?
- Do you want to arrange your own placement or would you rather have one that is arranged for you?
- Can you afford to do a placement that you have to fund yourself?
- How far do you wish to travel to do your placement?
- Do you want to be placed in a school where the main language is English?
- Do you want to experience a very different curriculum?
- If you are a student teacher, how will you ensure that you link your international placement to QTS?

Having considered these questions it may be that you would prefer a placement that is organized for you by your training provider and one that will attract some funding. If that is the case, your choice of placement will be limited to Europe and to countries where your provider has links. This still allows for a considerable amount of choice.

The following case studies are from two students who completed 3-week placements under the Leonardo programme in Finland.

Case Study A

I think it is important to sample as much of each of the school years from Kindergarten upwards, as is possible. Rather than just sitting back and observing, I have enjoyed getting in among the children who have only been too happy to show me their work. My experience on this placement has also been that teachers are more than happy to answer questions, even briefly breaking off their teaching, especially if something is being taught which I was not sure of.

The teachers were my primary source of language translation. There was also a program on my teacher's computer that would translate a word from English to Finnish, so I was able to produce a word list for myself. Also a couple of the children who could speak very good English became my unofficial translators when I was having problems communicating with a child near to them (which I am sure they enjoyed doing for me).

Case Study B

The linguistic and cultural preparation helped me to understand some of the customs and words in order to be polite. It meant that I was not so shocked with things such as the children removing their shoes in class, or saunas . . . It gave me an initial starting conversation when introduced to my family and an understanding of why there are such traditions.

The experience has given me more experience of teaching children with English as an additional language which will help me when faced with such a situation on placement and real life. I will use discussion more within lessons and I will value and feel empathy for children who speak more than one language and who may be struggling with English. In the future I will give the children more responsibility for their own work and I will try to use topic work more often as I feel it links the different subjects well.

As you read these experiences from students we hope that you will notice how they have benefited from their placements. For many students, the opportunities that alternative or international placements offer are life changing and if you have such an opportunity, take your time to choose the right placement for you and then enjoy it.

Key points

- There are many choices to be made and time will be needed to consider these thoroughly, before making a decision.
- You can express preferences when approaching a traditional placement but your training provider will not necessarily be able to meet them.
- A breadth of experience is useful when applying for jobs.
- Decide what you want to gain from an alternative placement and this will help you choose from the numerous opportunities.
- If you have funding, or the ability to fund, an international placement, this can be an amazing experience.
- All placements should enable you to reflect on pedagogical similarities and differences, as well as contributing to your development as a teacher.

Resources

www.britishcouncil.org/erasmus
www.leonardo.org.uk
www.teachers.tv/videos/teaching-practice
www.teachingoutsidetheclassroom.com

3

Preparation is a Key to Success

Summary

Before embarking on a placement, be it a traditional school experience, an alternative or an international placement, it is necessary to prepare as effectively and thoroughly as possible. The more focused, informed and meaningful the preparation you engage in, the more likelihood of a successful and enjoyable placement.

In this chapter we will explore some of the issues and considerations you will need to take into account as you plan and prepare for your placement. We will consider basic preparation for any placement, such as research and seeking out tutors or students who may have information about the placement you are going to. We will then highlight particular considerations for alternative placements; and explore in some depth, issues such as travel, accommodation and health and safety with regard to international placements.

Pre-placement preparation

We recommend that before you go on a placement, you should join a teaching union. There are many benefits such as support, guidance and advice, including legal advice. Union membership is normally offered free to students and some students join all the unions before deciding which one to join when they have to pay at the start of their teaching career. The unions are:

- Association of Teachers and Lecturers (ATL)
- National Association of Schoolmasters/Union of Women Teachers (NASUWT)
- National Union of Teachers (NUT)
- Voice

Most training providers invite the unions to some form of open day where you can register your membership. If this is not the case, then you can contact the unions directly. The websites for each of these unions are included in the resources section at the end of the chapter.

Traditional placements

As soon as a placement has been agreed you should begin your research.

- Search the internet to see if the school has a website, or if there are any articles or information about the school;
- request a prospectus or further information – some schools provide a student's guide;
- access reports from Ofsted and the Local Authority;
- talk to tutors and students about their experiences, if the school has hosted students before;
- locate the school, and if possible travel there and back during a working day, to see how long the journey will take and if there are potential issues with public transport, or parking;
- talk about car sharing or travelling together, if other students are going to the same placement, or a school near to yours;
- make preparation visits, and be vigilant, taking note of routines, behaviour management strategies, availability of resources and facilities;

- undertake observation tasks and activities set by your training provider;
- develop relationships with the children/students, staff and adults working in the school;
- offer to help in the class or school: make drinks, help tidy away, sort out cupboards (a good way to see what resources there are and to ask which you will be able to use);
- accompany the class or school on a trip (so that you have a chance to get to know the children and adults outside the school context);
- look after a stall at the school fair/fete (an excellent and informal way to meet parents and members of the local community, and to start to develop relationships before you start your placement);
- ask to be shown examples of school long, medium and short term planning; and clarify what you will be expected to teach and the planning you will need to produce during your placement;
- show your class teacher and mentor copies of your initial ideas for lessons and activities, and drafts of your planning, to check that these will be appropriate and acceptable before you produce too many;
- learn the children's names as soon as you can, as this will help to secure more successful relationships, and aid learning and teaching.

This early preparation should help to ensure that you have a good knowledge of the placement before you start, and will demonstrate to the staff at the school that you are keen, motivated, organized and able to use your initiative. Remember that every placement will be different, and as Carolyn discovered this required careful consideration, and recognition that previously held assumptions may not really be the case.

Case Study: Carolyn – Rural School

In my fourth year of teacher training, the University placed me in a rural primary school for my final block placement. The school was situated in the North West of England and served a small, close-knit village community. The school was small (only four classes) and thus had mixed-aged classes, where children spent 2 years in each class. Class 1 was for Nursery/Reception aged children, Class 2 was for Year 1/2, Class 3 was for Year 3/4, and Class 4 was for Year 5/6. I spent 8 weeks teaching Class 3, with children ranging from age 7 to 9. My class was full of white, middle class children – an unusual experience for me after spending much of my training teaching in multicultural, multiethnic and socioeconomically deprived areas. I had also never taught in a school that had been judged 'outstanding' by Ofsted: this one had.

Case Study—Cont'd

The University expected a lot from us on this placement, we had to prove we were ready for the teaching profession. I knew I had to perform well; this was the last hurdle before I qualified. If I did well I would graduate and be on my way to teaching my own class in September. If I didn't do so well, I would have to repeat the year. Seeing as so much hinged on whether I passed this placement, I was determined to do a good job. The fact that I was placed in what you would probably call a 'nice' school did ease my anxiety, but I was still aware I was expected to teach as good as a professional to pass. In addition, this was the first time the University would be grading my performance, and being the ambitious person that I am, I desperately wanted to be graded as a First.

So as I embarked on my 8 weeks of teaching in a rural school, I didn't initially think there would be many challenges getting in my way. After all, this was a 'nice' country school. I just had to teach my little socks off and everything would go swimmingly. However, I learnt from this placement that every school, in fact every class, has their own plethora of issues that as a teacher you need to accommodate and plan for. It isn't about you just teaching a class, it's about accommodating every individual in that class.

As a starting point I quickly identified the following challenges I would have to meet:

Planning and teaching for a mixed-age class;
teaching in an inclusive way which would cater for the needs of two children with hearing impairments;
managing the behaviour of two age groups within one class;
learning how to operate as a school within a community and how to get involved with members of it.

Consider:

- How could Carolyn begin to address the four challenges that she set herself at the beginning of the placement?
- When you have confirmed your placement what will be some of the challenges that you set for yourself?

Alternative placements

After giving careful thought to where you want your alternative placement to be, and securing a place there, you need to prepare as thoroughly as possible. Alternative placements are not the 'easy' option; they are different to traditional placements and possibly unique to your training provider, and in many ways this will necessitate extra preparation.

- Search the internet to see if the setting has its own website, or if there are any articles or information about the setting;
- research the area or setting in libraries, journals or books;

- contact the setting and ask if you can make a preliminary visit, if this is feasible in terms of distance and time. If not, ask the setting if they can send you any useful information, or direct you to where this can be found;
- establish clear outcomes and objectives for the placement, for you and the setting, as these will be different, and try to link these to QTS when appropriate;
- ensure that you know what is expected of you by your training provider and the setting, and talk to your link contact if there appears to be potentially diverse expectations;
- ask to be shown relevant planning; and clarify what you will be expected to plan before and during your placement;
- show setting staff copies of your initial ideas for lessons and activities, and drafts of your planning, to ascertain that these will be appropriate and acceptable.

In Chapter 1 we considered Carolyn's initial reaction when she was about to start her alternative placement in an art gallery. We now consider her preparation. Carolyn realized that this would be a very different experience from previous ones and would involve a significant amount of work!

Case Study: Carolyn – Art Gallery

As the panic set in it was clear that the first thing I had to do was establish placement objectives for myself and the host. I did this by having a lengthy discussion with the education officer at the gallery about exactly what each of us wanted to gain from the placement. We hoped this would ensure that my time spent at the gallery would be focused and successful from the outset, with positive outcomes for myself as a student teacher and the gallery as an alternative educational setting.

We established the following objectives for the host:

To develop stronger links with the formal educational world;
To find out about current issues and needs for schools, teachers and pupils;
To improve provision at the gallery for schools.

We agreed on the following objectives for me:

To gain confidence in using outside resources (i.e., the gallery) to enhance children's learning;
To develop art subject knowledge and how to use it to enhance other curriculum subjects;
To increase the use of creativity in teaching;
To increase cross curricular links in planning and teaching.

Case Study—Cont'd

Once the placement objectives had been established I felt more confident about what I wanted to achieve during the placement. In turn, this kick started the planning process, since I was now focused on examining, exploring and exploiting cross-curricular, creative approaches to teaching by utilising the resources in this setting. I began by assisting the education officer with the school workshops the gallery already had in place. This taught me how learning experiences for all ages and abilities could be created around pieces of artwork in the gallery. It enlightened me to the learning power held in pieces of real-life art work – children from early years through to Key Stage 3 appeared to find the paintings and sculptures completely engaging and compelling. This was the most important thing I learnt about planning, that it should be focused around something visual in order to engage the interest of the learners and it should incorporate practical, kinaesthetic elements which build on this visual stimulus.

Consider:

- Why is it important to discuss and agree your objectives, and those of the host, before you start the placement?
- What can you plan before the placement starts, and will this be dependent on information from the host? If so, how might you request this?

International placements

If you are fortunate enough to be able to undertake an international placement then appropriate preparation prior to travel is vital. You will need to keep an open mind, be flexible, adaptable, resistant and eager to learn and discover new ideas, beliefs and ideologies; and to expect the unexpected. Investigate the education system of the host country you are due to visit as this will have a huge impact on the provision there.

- Is there 'free' education for all children?
- What percentage of the children attend school?
- How is the education and school system structured?

Gaining background knowledge and understanding will help ensure that you gain a context for the placement.

Adelle was offered the opportunity to engage in a placement in two schools in America, which she relished. She recognized that gaining relevant information and making contacts in preparation for the visit would be fundamental in ensuring that the placement was a positive one.

Case Study: Adelle – America

During our time in Holland in Michigan, America we were placed in two schools, Van Raalte and Woodside Elementary. These schools both draw from a similar catchment area, mostly Hispanic and white Americans and classed as economically disadvantaged.

I found out a little about the area I was going to and Uni was great in offering us a buddy system, where we could contact a student teacher who was kind enough to share their experiences with me. This enabled us to ask them what resources they had in the schools, what they thought we should take out there to share with the children and if they had any top tips for us. During the planning process both universities were a great help and offered lots of support and guidance. The moment we got to America we were given even more information about the schools, what we should expect, even down to what questions the children were wanting and liable to ask.

Resources for this type of placement were really everyday resources that you would use in schools in England. When talking with my buddy, she wanted to know the basics about what we had in our schools and were they the same as they used. This also applied to the children; they wanted to know what we had for our classes and what the children looked like, etc. So on the outward journey, the suitcase was filled with story books, stickers, labels, posters, exercise books, pictures, all the things that you would expect to have in an English school. These are what the children and staff wanted to see, real life things, not just pictures from an old book. When planning, the most important thing I learned was to ask the children and the staff what they would like to know and see, from there the planning was easy.

Consider:

- Can you produce a list of resources that you could take to your placement?
- Are there resources that you could usefully develop before the placement starts?

Ethical considerations

Whenever you work with children and young adults you need to take into account potential ethical issues. At a fundamental level this could be ensuring that you have an up-to-date Criminal Records Bureau (CRB) check and have a recorded number to demonstrate this.

Further information can be found at www.crb.homeoffice.gov.uk/. It might be ensuring that you have gained permission from the child, parent, teacher, head teacher (as appropriate) to take photographs and to record evidence. Each school and setting will have their own guidelines and requirements, and you need to be aware and comply with these.

However you may encounter more complex and potentially difficult ethical issues, irrespective of whether your placement is traditional, alternative or international. The role of children in society may be significantly different from the one you have experienced to date. The economic, political, cultural and social situation may mean that there are limited opportunities for education, and few schools and teachers, in a particular area. Maybe parents/adults are unable to afford to send children to schools, where 'free' education is not available. In a country, situation or area where starvation, dehydration and disease are endemic, then the priority will be survival, and education may be a long distant aspiration. Children may need to work from an early age to support their family and themselves, or 'human rights' may not be perceived in the way you might expect. In such a context, corporal punishment as a behaviour management strategy, for example, may be the rule rather than the exception.

At an alternative extreme you may be working in a particularly affluent country, area, school or setting. Parents and guardians may be funding their child's education at considerable expense. The expectations of the children, students, staff and parents may be different from those you have experienced before. For example, there may be pressure to ensure that all the children and students gain very high grades; or participate in many extra curricular activities, which teachers and staff at the school or setting are actively engaged in.

It is important to be aware of any religious and cultural issues that are relevant to your placement. If you are placed in a faith school it is important to find out if there are any particular expectations of you. For example, you may be expected to lead prayers before lunch and at the end of the day. As a teacher, you understand this before you apply to teach in a faith school but, as a student, you are often placed where your training provider finds a placement. You need to tell your training provider if being placed in any faith school causes you concern.

On an international placement, you may be unfamiliar with the religious or cultural customs of the country. It is important to find out as much as you can about the dominant religion, or religions, so that you can show appropriate respect and not offend anyone unintentionally. Your training provider and staff at the placement setting will be able to advise you. Gaining some knowledge and understanding of the country, region, location and particular setting should help to alleviate potential problems and reassure family and friends back at home. Even a basic knowledge of the history and development of the country, situation and setting, will give you a more informed contextual understanding. Some understanding of the past will also prove useful as you try to interpret the present and proceed into the future.

Health and safety

In the excitement of preparing for your placement you may give limited consideration to health and safety issues, but being aware of these and planning ahead should help to ensure that the experience is a positive one.

Depending on where your placement is to be undertaken a risk assessment may need to be carried out. Check with your training provider to see if one is needed or has already been done. This could involve a visit to the setting by the training provider to check that appropriate health and safety guidelines and requirements have been followed. This is particularly significant if your placement is being carried out in an alternative setting such as an outdoor education centre, or a children's farm or a museum, or if you have a disability or specific need that needs to be accommodated. Alternatively, you may be asked to check health and safety issues and requirements directly with the setting, and to ensure that the placement will be a safe and appropriate one.

You need to be self aware and proactive, especially when opting for alternative and international placements, as you are undertaking a different kind of experience. Adopting a positive, engaged, responsible and informed attitude, rather than naively engaging in something you know little about with limited preparation, knowledge or understanding, will be influential in determining the outcome of the placement. If travelling abroad, check the Foreign and Commonwealth Office and specific embassy guidance and recommendations (as detailed in subsequent sections), before finalizing the placement. Ensure that you have travel insurance and that this will cover you for all eventualities, taking care to note any exceptions to cover, such as various sporting and recreational activities.

Initially you should contact organizations and find specific information for the country you are going to undertake your placement in, such as:

Foreign and Commonwealth Office

www.fco.gov.uk/en/travel-and-living-abroad/travel-advice-by-country/

This site will also provide links to relevant foreign embassies and the London Diplomatic list:

www.fco.gov.uk/resources/en/protocol/ldl-August2010

The Foreign and Commonwealth Office website provides guidance on travel, and living abroad, for a significant number of countries. It also has updated travel news, passport and visa advice and entry requirements. The website also provides information on 'Staying safe and healthy', which includes a travel checklist; travel health; travel insurance advice; driving abroad; travel money; eat and drink safely; tropical cyclones; terrorism; river and sea safety including piracy; and when things go wrong.

You should take out insurance before you travel, to cover the whole of the time you will be abroad. Applying for The European Health Insurance Card (EHIC) would also be useful. The card gives you rights to health care during a temporary visit to European Economic Area (EEA) countries or Switzerland. Anyone, aged 16 or over, who are normally resident in the UK can apply for an EHIC. There may be some restrictions depending on your nationality – visit the Department of Health website for more info about who is eligible. If you are travelling as a group, each person in the group requires a card. If you have an EHIC and you have an accident or suddenly become ill you will receive the necessary state-provided medical health care for a reduced cost, or sometimes free. You will be treated on the same terms as insured nationals of the country you are visiting. However the card will not cover all your medical costs or private treatment, or repatriation to the UK. Also overseas state-provided health care may not cover entitlements you may receive for free on the NHS. So you will still need appropriate insurance to ensure you are fully covered for all eventualities during your travel and stay.

Many people think an EHIC will be enough and don't take out insurance. They regret this when they have to pay thousands of pounds for an air ambulance back to the UK or pay out for extra accommodation to stay with a sick relative. (www.fco.gov.uk/en/travel-and-living-abroad/travel-advice-by-country/)

To apply for your EHIC contact the Department of Health or European Health Insurance Card:

- phone 0845 606 2030 or
- complete the application form available from some Post Offices and post it using the accompanying addressed envelope.

The Department of Health website

www.nhs.uk/nhsengland/Healthcareabroad/pages/Healthcareabroad.aspx

This site includes details of medical health care abroad including medical health care insurance, which you should arrange and take out before you travel, in addition to the EHIC.

Travel

Take time and advice before making travel arrangements. You will need to confirm exact dates with your training provider. If you are going on a traditional or a local alternative experience the school or setting may expect you to make preparatory visits before you start the actual placement, in which case, you will need to make travel arrangements for these days, as well as the placement dates.

If you are travelling abroad then the need to ensure you have appropriate travel arrangements is vitally important. There are many 'cheap' or 'economy' airlines, which initially may appear to be a 'bargain', but take care before you book. Most economy airlines add tax to each journey, which is often more expensive than the actual flight, and can make a reasonable journey fairly expensive. Many economy airlines also make additional charges for luggage, suitcases to be put in the hold and hand luggage to be taken on the airplane. Charges are also made for meals that you have during the journey, if you want to pre-book a seat and if you want to guarantee a seat next to another traveller. All these additional extras can mount up, so it is worth comparing the overall cost. Comparison websites could prove useful in comparing costs across a range of airlines.

Customs control at airports and boat and ferry ports are increasingly stringent about what you are allowed to take in and out of different countries. All airports do not permit sharp objects in hand luggage, so you would be unable to pack scissors or craft knives etc. in a holdall that you would be taking onto the aeroplane. There are also specific regulations with regard to liquids and foodstuffs. So you need to check with your airline and airport before you travel, and ensure that you know what can and cannot be packed in hand and hold luggage. Most airlines have specific restrictions on the amount and weight of hand and hold luggage that you are permitted to take. If you go over these limits you will be charged per kilo for the additional weight, which can prove very expensive. Remember that you may want to bring souvenirs or gifts from your overseas experience, so you will need to keep some space and weight limit for the return journey unless you intend to leave most of your clothes, towels, footwear and so on behind to be recycled or used again.

If you normally book 'a package' with a travel agent when you go on holiday, this will normally be 'ATOL' bonded. ATOL is a financial protection scheme managed by the Civil Aviation Authority ('CAA'). All travel companies selling air holiday packages and flights in the UK are required by law to hold a licence called an Air Travel Organizer's Licence ('ATOL'), which is granted after the company has met the CAA's licensing requirements. (Refer to the Civil Aviation Authority – www.caa.co.uk/). If the holiday company or airline or accommodation should go into liquidation you would be able to apply for a refund. However, if you book each part of your arrangements separately on the internet these are less likely to be ATOL bonded and you may neither be able to claim a refund nor be offered alternative arrangements. If you pay for travel, accommodation and transfers with a credit card then you may be able to claim from them, but this depends on the credit card company and you need to check this before booking.

Accommodation

One of the most important decisions you will need to make is where you will be living during the placement. If the placement is located far from 'home' then you may decide to find temporary accommodation, rather than travelling back and forth every day. A relatively simple solution may be to live with relatives or friends, who are closer to your placement. However, remember that there could be different house rules and customs, compared with the ones you may be used to.

If you are going abroad then there are a number of options available. You could live in halls of residence at the partner training provider, sometimes arranged for you with Erasmus and Leonardo programmes. Alternatively, you could live in the home of a 'host' or 'host family'. This has the amazing benefit of experiencing real local life, and gaining firsthand experience of local customs and traditions.

Being a responsible tourist and visitor

Although you will be on a placement, you will still be a tourist and a visitor in any setting you undertake your placement in, so you should recognize the need to make responsible choices while you are there. Common-sense examples such as turning taps off when they have been left on in school, recycling as many materials as possible and encouraging the children and other adults to do the same. However when you travel further afield you should be aware of the communities, location and environment around you.

The 'Know Before You Go' (KBYG) is an ongoing campaign with around 400 travel industry partners designed to help you to stay safe and healthy abroad.

The campaign was launched in 2001 to promote these key messages:

- get adequate travel insurance
- check the Foreign and Commonwealth Office country travel advice
- research your destination – know the local laws and customs
- visit your GP as soon as possible before travelling
- check your passport is in good condition and valid and you have all necessary visas
- make copies of important travel documents and/or store them online using a secure data storage site
- tell someone where you are going and leave emergency contact details with them
- take enough money and have access to emergency funds

Every year thousands of British travellers seriously regret not taking these simple steps. If you're planning a trip you should read the travellers checklist – it's full of practical tips for having a safe and enjoyable time.

Our research has shown that particular groups of travellers experience unique problems. We use mini-campaigns to reach these groups with our advice:

- independent travellers
- single-sex groups
- package holiday-makers
- gap year travellers
- sports travellers
- people visiting friends and family
- elderly and retired travellers

For example, younger travellers are the least prepared group of UK travellers – that's why we launched the dedicated GoGapYear.com website and work with specialist travel companies and universities to get our message to them. (www.fco.gov.uk/travel)

If you are a British national, and travelling or living abroad, or planning to do so, you can register with the 'LOCATE' service.

We are encouraging all British nationals travelling and living abroad to register with us on LOCATE, even for short trips. What are the benefits of registering with LOCATE?

- if a major catastrophe occurs we'll have an instant record of your details so we can contact you to make sure you're OK and provide advice;
- if family and friends need to get in touch with you we can help them to find you;
- it only takes a few minutes to register your travel or residence information online and the local British Embassy will know you are coming. You do not need to contact them directly;
- you only need to register for the service once and then update your account when you make a new trip abroad or change your country of residence. You can even add planned trips abroad up to a year ahead;
- LOCATE improves our ability to provide help in an emergency and reduce delay and worry in times of stress for family and friends at home (www.locate.fco.gov.uk/locateportal/).

Contacts

You should ensure that your family, friends and training provider have full details of your contact address, telephone number and email account, before you travel. If you move to a different location remember to update this information. You should aim to keep in regular contact so that those back at home know that you are safe and that you do not have any problems or concerns. Contact your mentor at the placement and/or your link contact if there are any issues during the placement, and make sure they have your email address so they can contact you.

Unfortunately problems can occur while on any placement, so let your mentor, teacher and training provider know as soon as possible, so that they can advise and support you. If the issue is an emergency and you are abroad you may also need to contact the local embassy for support and guidance. If you become a victim of a crime, or fall seriously ill, or have another serious problem you can contact the Consular Assistance team in London on 020 7008 1500 (+44 20 7008 1500 from abroad). This number operates 24 hours a day (www.fco.gov.uk/en/travel-and-living-abroad/when-things-go-wrong/).

Induction programmes

Training providers may organize an induction programme or a number of induction events, in preparation for your placement abroad. These may include generic sessions to ensure that you know what arrangements you need to make in terms of travel, accommodation, insurance, health and safety, applicable to anyone travelling to another country. You may also have specific sessions concerned with ensuring that you have details of the school, staff, contact details and focused preparation depending on the country and setting you will have your placement in.

There may be cultural induction sessions, where you attend local community events and gain knowledge and understanding of diverse cultural expectations and norms. This could involve advice on buying or loaning traditional dress, for specific events you may be expected to attend, such as a sari if you are going to attend events while doing a placement in India. Or there could be the offer of language classes, so that you have a basic knowledge of useful words and phrases.

Meetings with foreign students and visitors

Your training provider may host students from other countries on various exchange, Erasmus or Leonardo programmes. You should contact the International Co-ordinator, or equivalent person, and ask if there are any students from the country you are visiting; or if they have any links with people in that country who you could contact for information and advice prior to travel. If there are foreign students in your institution, arrange to meet them, and ask them to tell you about life, education and schools in their home country. They may enjoy the opportunity to talk to you about 'home', to be the 'expert' and give advice and guidance, and to practice their English language skills on a receptive and grateful audience! They may also be prepared to offer language tuition, which could be organized through the International Co-ordinator.

Meetings with students and teachers

Training providers often ask former students and teachers to return to talk about their placements and experiences. If such events are organized make every effort to attend as these are really useful and motivating. You can normally ask questions that you may not want to ask tutors, and get 'real life' responses. If your training provider does not provide this opportunity then take the initiative and ask if you can arrange such a session, or a meeting. This could also provide further evidence of you meeting the QTS standards.

The training provider would need to pass on your email contact to an appropriate person, for them to contact you, but this should be possible. One step further would be to become part of, or start, a 'buddy' system, where you are paired with a student or teacher who has already undertaken a placement in a similar setting and situation, or in the same country, area and location. The buddy system would enable you to gain specific and focused guidance before, during and after your placement, and hopefully gain a new friend and colleague.

Key points

- Preparation is essential for success.
- Find out as much as you can about the school, setting, location and country before you start the placement.
- Contact tutors, students and teachers who have visited or worked in the school, setting, location and country before and can provide invaluable advice, guidance and support.
- There are many ethical issues involved in working with children and students, which need to be carefully considered before, during and after your placement.
- Ensure that you follow health and safety advice, to ensure that you have the best chance of an enjoyable and problem free experience.
- Arrange travel well in advance, with a reputable ATOL and ABTA bonded company.
- Review accommodation choices, and make an informed decision based on your particular circumstances.

Resources

www.crb.homeoffice.gov.uk
www.ofsted.gov.uk
www.teachernet.gov.uk
www.teachers.tv/videos/teaching-practice/

The Department of Health website
www.nhs.uk/nhsengland/Healthcareabroad/pages/Healthcareabroad.aspx

Foreign and Commonwealth Office
www.fco.gov.uk/en/travel-and-living-abroad/travel-advice-by-country/

Civil Aviation Authority
www.caa.co.uk

National Union of Teachers

www.teachers.org.uk

National Association of Schoolmasters / Union of Women Teachers

www.teachersunion.org.uk

Association of Teachers and Lecturers

www.askatl.org.uk

Voice Union the Education Professionals

www.voicetheunion.org.uk

Part II
Your Placement

Make the Most of Every Situation

Summary

You will have diverse hopes, aspirations, intentions and expectations, as you plan and prepare for your placement. Fundamentally you will want to have a positive, meaningful and enjoyable experience that provides the chance to grow and develop as a person and a professional. In order to achieve this you should aim to make the most of every situation and opportunity that arise before, during and after your placement, as well as reflect on and evaluate such situations.

In this chapter we will investigate the need to gain background knowledge of the situational, cultural and religious context of your placement, irrespective of whether it will be traditional, alternative or international. The more information you can glean before you set off, the better prepared you will be. During the placement itself, take opportunities to travel, meet local people and visit places of interest and significance to that location. This will make your placement even more valuable, insightful and provide many stories and memories to share with others.

Situational knowledge

The more research you can do prior to your placement the more beneficial to your experience. An effective background knowledge of the historical, geographical and cultural development of the area and the school or setting will mean that you have a better understanding of the situational context of your placement. Your training provider, library and internet are a useful starting place. We would recommend keeping a journal, or more specifically a 'learning journal', from the day you find out where your placement will be. You can add information that you find out, so that it is accessible and in one place, but also to track your thoughts and ideas as your preparation gains momentum. You will be constructing a very useful portfolio which could be utilized in job interviews, or in assessed work. Once you are in the setting and the placement starts you will be able to record an account of what you have done each day, to reflect on this and to consider and analyse.

Keeping a 'learning journal'

A 'learning journal' can be a notebook, a file or a memory stick that contains your notes for each day, and significantly your reflections on these and a resultant analysis or commentary, so that your learning is enhanced. Keeping a journal will help you to remember each day and allow you to go back, reflect and consider. It will help you to monitor your experience and to track the highs and lows, your strengths and areas for development, but also to consider the why and what for? A journal allows us time to take a step back, and to reflect on what we have written and to think 'did I really do that? Why?!'

Smith (2006) states:

> Writing things down in a journal also allows us to 'clear our minds'. Having made a note of something we can put them on one side for consideration or action at a later point. We can only handle so much at any one moment. Trying to remember this or that, and deal with current situations, can sometimes mean that we are not focusing on what we need to. As Mary Louise Holly (1989: 9) again puts it, 'The journal offers a way to sort out the multitude of demands and interactions and to highlight the most important ones'. Last, and certainly not least, making journal writing part of our routine means that we do actually take time out to reflect on what might be happening in our practice and in our lives generally (Rainer 2004). From this we can see that writing and keeping a journal holds the possibility of deepening our self-understanding, and to making added sense of our lives and what we believe (www.infed.org/research/keeping_a_journal.htm).

Klug (2002) in Smith (2006) developed a list of potential starter questions to stimulate ideas for writing a journal each day.

- As I look back on the day, what were the most significant events?
- In what ways was this day unique, different from other days?
- Did I have any particularly meaningful conversations?
- Did I do any reading? What were my reactions to it?

- How did I feel during the day? What were the emotional highs and lows? Why did I feel as I did?
- Did I find myself worrying about anything today?
- What were the chief joys of the day? What did I accomplish?
- Did I fail at anything? What can I learn from this?
- What did I learn today?

Lastly, it is important to be honest when writing journals. Write how you really feel and not how you think you *should* feel. Record what you really think, not what you believe you *ought* to think (pp 54–56).

Gaining information and making contacts
Once you have gained some background information about the location and the setting, you need to start to 'dig' deeper and gain more tangible knowledge and understanding.

Potential sources of information include:

- Tutors, students and teachers who have knowledge of the location and setting;
- Students who have already undertaken a placement in a particular school, setting, area or country;
- Members of the community with knowledge of an area or setting;
- Community leaders and organizations with specific links to the area or setting;
- Experts with a detailed knowledge of a specific location or area, or type of setting;
- Erasmus, exchange and foreign students and teachers;
- Language and cultural sessions.

If you can talk to someone who has been to a particular school, setting, location or country before, and they are willing to share their experiences, then accept their offer, listen, make notes (perhaps in a journal) and ask lots of questions! If they know people in the school, setting, location or country that would be willing for you to contact them before and during your placement, then this would be a very proactive way of making situational links.

Rachel was part of a group of teachers and students who travelled to the Gambia, West Africa, for an international placement. Tutors, students and teachers who had previously travelled and worked in schools and nurseries in the Gambia were keen to share their experiences and give advice and support, which was taken on board by the students when preparing for the placement. It is vital that students undertaking placements in developing countries should be as prepared as possible before travelling. Even with thorough preparation, and a background knowledge of the setting, area, location and local community, Rachel's experience proved to be an 'eye opening' and surprising one, from the first day of arrival into the small village in West Africa.

Case Study: Rachel – Gambia

In February, when I visited it was 43°c. Each day children walked to school in very hot weather and then sat in cramped hot classrooms; which could adversely affect their mood, concentration and ability to learn. There was an average of 46 children per class, and they sat four or five to a desk. They were crammed together creating an uncomfortable environment in which to learn. It was difficult for the children to learn in such poor, crowded conditions. Many children preferred sitting on the floor closer to the board (a black painted wall) as the classrooms were so dark it was hard to see what the teacher had written. The lack of light in the classrooms was a key issue in Gambia. There were small holes in the wall and no electricity for lighting; this had an immediate effect on the children's ability to learn.

Consider:

- How might you feel in, or respond to, a similar situation?
- How can you prepare for such a diverse experience?

Cultural knowledge

Through your background research you should be able to gain some cultural knowledge of the setting, and location. Within any setting there may be children and adults with a variety of cultural beliefs and practices. Cultural beliefs should not be mistaken for religious beliefs, which are discussed later in the chapter. So what is culture? There are many different definitions and meanings of culture, which could be useful to explore. However we will focus on a generic definition of culture as a set of shared attitudes, values, goals and practices that characterizes a setting, a location, a group or a community. Thus developing a cultural knowledge of the setting and location for your placement will involve investigating the people within it, and their attitudes, values, norms and practices. However, be mindful not to over generalize as within any culture there may be different belief systems and philosophies. The culture of a setting or an area will vary from place to place, and there will be a unique culture to each placement setting. Some settings will be culturally similar to those you may have experienced before; others may be fundamentally different, especially if you undertake an international placement.

Making cultural links

One of the key factors in a positive international placement is the cultural preparation and induction that you should be willing to immerse yourself in even before your flight takes off. As stated in Chapter 3 your training provider may arrange for you to undertake visits to a local community and may have established links with local cultural leaders. They may organize meetings with members of the local community that have experience of the country or area you are travelling to. If your training provider is unable to do this then you could do this independently. The importance of this cannot be stressed more strongly. Students and teachers who have participated in placements abroad note that cultural preparation is vital to the success and enjoyment of the placement.

There may be cultural attitudes, norms and practices which you are unaware of, and you could potentially cause offence without intending to. The best way to try to avoid this is to find out as much as you can before you travel, and to be polite and observant during the placement. Do your hosts take off their shoes before entering a room? If yes, then you should do similarly. When eating meals does one particular person start before the others? If you are offered goat, which may be a local delicacy, how do you respond? Offending without intention can be difficult to deal with, so pre-empt and discuss possible issues and problems before they arise, to avoid embarrassment, discomfort and challenging situations.

Packing your suitcase before travel is a necessity, but can be exciting as it means that the journey and experience will start soon, and hopefully you will be eager with anticipation. However, you will need to give some thought to this, and perhaps seek advice. You may be travelling to the Gambia, and it may be 40 degrees in the shade, but would a vest top and shorts be suitable when teaching in the local school? If you take into account the cultural beliefs and expectations, would this be acceptable or perhaps offensive and possibly perceived as disrespectful? You will need cool clothes because of the heat, but these should be appropriate to the setting and culture your placement is in. Some countries are very hot and humid during the day, but can be cool in the evenings, so you may need to be prepared for this on a practical level, but also on a personal and professional level.

Despite meeting with a number of Japanese exchange students, and reading and researching Japanese culture and customs, David found that it was not until he was in school, that the repercussions of different culture and customs became more apparent.

Case Study: David – Japan

Although at first a mystery and then slightly puzzling, once I began to understand not just the school context but the cultural context, then the intricacies of the classroom behaviour and management became much clearer. This was a culture where there was a significant emphasis on the group mentality compared to the individual. The notion of group mentality began from day one of a child's peer to peer experiences. This was reflected in the children discussing and solving problems within their class environment and the teacher merely being an overseer in personal, social and emotional terms. Although, undoubtedly, there were occasions when teachers did intervene, these tended to be minimal compared to England.

Classroom and behaviour management were my most challenging puzzle during my placement in a Japanese school, as it was so indirect and therefore hard to identify at first. It was only after a week of observations, many questions and background reading that I began to understand how it worked. It was the children themselves who were given the responsibility for managing each others' behaviour. There was very little direct input from the teacher. The formalities that began and ended each lesson were a clear indicator of what sort of behaviour was expected from the children. The children who begin the formalities at the beginning of the lesson did not begin until everyone is ready, sometimes this meant they would go and confront a child who was not ready to see what the problem was.

During lunch and break recess children were left to their own devices, which often involved roaming around the whole of the school grounds, seen or unseen. Most lessons were followed by a ten minute recess, where the children usually remained in the classroom. During one such recess I witnessed a fight break out, the teacher was sat at the front of the classroom marking work and ignored it. Class children split the fight up and spoke to each of the individuals involved. When the next lesson began, the teacher enquired as to whether things had been sorted out, both individuals agreed it had and the lesson continued with nothing else said. Here, the classmates had felt it their responsibility to stop, rather than encourage, the fight that started in the class. This promotion of independence was something that seemed natural to both the children and the adults.

Another strategy that I saw widely used was 'Jan-ken', or as known in English, 'paper, rock, scissors'. I was amazed at the efficiency of using such a simple game to sort out problems and choose people. For example, if children were arguing over something, they would play Jan-ken to decide who got it. There was no room for discussion after Jan-ken had taken place, whoever lost, lost. I also saw it used when the teacher was choosing the children for different parts in a play. The children could not decide who was who, so the teacher said the part and then asked the children who wanted

Case Study—Cont'd

that part to stand up and play group Jan-ken until there was only one person left for the part. I asked the teachers whether the best dramatists had the lead roles, they laughed and said no, why should they?

Consider:

- What has been the role of culture in schools and settings with which you are familiar?
- What impact may different cultural expectations and values have on learning and teaching in a particular school or setting?

Religious knowledge

Religion and culture can be fundamentally different. As discussed, culture focuses on shared attitudes, values, goals and practices that characterize a setting, a location, a group or a community. These can differ from person to person, setting to setting, community to community, due to religious beliefs and practices. When preparing to undertake a placement to India a group of students visited a local temple, met with religious leaders in the local community and purchased traditional outfits to wear to events while in India. They were hosted by families in their homes and participated in traditional feasts and celebrations, learnt basic phrases and words and gained knowledge of the customs and beliefs of the area they were to visit. However, while undertaking their actual placement, they worked with adults and children with different religious beliefs and customs, which had a significant impact on their attitude and practices. The possibility that there may be diverse religious groups and customs within any setting, or area, needs to be considered and prepared for.

Gaining knowledge of distinct religious beliefs and traditions will prove useful for your professional development, irrespective of the type or location of your placements. It is useful to encourage pupils to gain knowledge of world religions and beliefs, and by developing your own knowledge you can become more aware and understanding of others. If your placement is in a faith school, do you know what the potential differences there may be compared with a non-faith school? If you are a non-Catholic, with a placement in a Catholic school, what do you do when the children say prayers and bless themselves before and after prayer? You may need to discuss this with your mentor in school, and ascertain what the expectations are and your role in this. If there are potential issues you need to mention this to a tutor from your training provider, so that resolutions can be made and agreed.

Mission statements

The mission statement of a school or setting is, by its very nature, a significant document, which should help you to gain a meaningful insight. The realization, or not, of the mission statement will become more apparent as your placement progresses. Before Rachel started her placement she researched education in the Gambia and noted that education was not compulsory, although it was recommended. Rachel knew that a situation where education was not compulsory would be significantly different from her own experiences of compulsory, 'free' education in England. This was reinforced when she read the mission statement for the school.

Case Study: Rachel – Gambia

The Lower Basic primary school that I undertook my international placement in was built in 1980 by the Charity SOS. The Charity has established schools and centres in Bakoteh, in the Gambia, to help provide the children with a basic education.

The Mission on which my placement school was based was displayed in the school:

School Mission

To cultivate in the children an interest in learning and to develop the skills needed in learning.

To encourage pupils to be interested generally in agriculture with emphasis on vegetable gardening, tree planting and flower growing, to beautify the school environment.

To demonstrate and maintain a high sense of discipline in and out of school.

The Mission included behaviour and learning objectives which are common to schools in England, however it also included specific reference to the environment and horticulture, demonstrating the importance of both.

Consider:

- What might the 'hidden messages' be behind such a Mission Statement?
- How could this impact on learning and teaching in the school?

Adapting to different situations

Every school and setting will be unique. You can have placements in two schools which are next to each other in terms of location, but they will have fundamental differences. The physical spaces, resources and facilities will vary; the policies, rules and routines will differ; and most significantly the adults and children are distinct individuals with their own thoughts, ideas, personalities and characters. All such characteristics and features may be referred to as the 'hidden curriculum', as discussed in Chapter 5. This is what is learnt by pupils and staff, but not necessarily planned for. This diversity necessitates that you keep an open mind, expect the unexpected and be willing to adapt to changes.

Consider the following extracts and consider what your reaction and response would be:

- You have been allocated a placement in a large urban school for your second placement; next to the school you undertook your first placement in. You speak to the placement co-ordinator and say that you have already been to a school in the same area, and that the school will be the same. The placement co-ordinator explains that she knows both schools well, and that you will have a very different experience. You can respond in various ways to these situations.
- During your first preparatory visit you meet the head teacher who tells you about the school. Do you say that you know all about the area already as your last placement was in the next school, or listen carefully for any new information that may be useful?
- You meet the class teacher you will be working with and he shows you some medium and short term planning and the templates that he would like you to use for your planning. Do you respond that it is not the same as the planning you did before and you would rather do it your way? Or do you say that the planning is very interesting, a variation on your previous planning, and it will be good to plan in a slightly different way?
- While in the staff room you are discussing displays in the school with another student and your mentor. You have noticed that some of the displays are fairly dated and ripped round the edges. Do you say that on your last placement they really cared about the learning environment and all the displays were really good? Or do you ask the mentor about the displays and volunteer to help with them when they are changed?

The examples should help to illustrate that your reaction to something that is different should not be one of comparison or panic, but rather a demonstration that you are willing to adapt to change in a positive and enthusiastic way. Remember there is not a right way and a wrong way – just many diverse ways!

Different teaching strategies

Jaz and Emma pioneered a first international placement to India, for their training provider. From discussions with tutors and teachers, who had experience working in schools in India, Jaz and Emma knew that the teaching strategies used, especially for their specialist subject, art; they were most likely be traditional. As part of the placement they hoped to be able to complete an art based project, which would encourage the children to be more active and independent. This would be fundamentally different from the usual art based work, which tended to focus on the teacher drawing something on the chalk board and the children copying it.

Case Study: Jaz – India

As a part of this international experience I, along with another student, proposed a mural project to promote a varied experience in art for the children. This project aimed to provide children with ownership of their artistic processes, which would be valued in a whole school context. This project was very different from what children had done before. As teachers, we provided guidance and choices as well as the freedom to explore a new medium (paint) to create art. By actually taking risks in creating something new and personal, children engaged in an artistic process rather than focusing on the end result.

While teachers were initially reticent about this project, as it progressed, it made them aware of the value of art. By observing the process, teachers commented that they learned about the value of teaching the skills and processes of art while nurturing the children within the whole learning environment. This project inspired teachers to develop their own projects and to collaborate with others. Significantly, they began to involve children in activities around the school (outside of the classroom) to promote experiential learning.

Consider:

- Jaz noted that art lessons were much more structured than he was used to, and thought that it would be useful to share his specialist interest in art with the children and staff. Why would he have needed to be careful when suggesting the project?
- What does the case study illustrate about achieving a positive placement?

During his placement in Japan, David noticed that there were very different teaching strategies compared with the ones he had experienced in settings in England, which reflected the culture, beliefs and practices of the situation.

Case Study: David – Japan

When children enter elementary school they can generally read and write, this is something that is usually taught on a one-to-one basis by the parents. By the end of the first grade children are expected to have learnt between seventy and eighty kanji. Japanese elementary schools are structurally very similar having virtually the same classroom set up through grades one to six. Japanese and Mathematics are taught everyday, with music, art and PE being taught frequently. Shodo (Japanese calligraphy) is taught from first grade progressing from pencil to paintbrush further up the school. Moral Studies is the equivalent of RE, which makes the children think of right and wrong contextual decisions but is devoid of any direct religious ethics. In the three weeks I spent in my main elementary school I only saw one visit to the computer room where the focus of the lesson was a maths game.

The most striking thing in elementary school was the difference between lesson time and recess time. There was at least ten minutes recess in between every period, during this time it was common to see children running, shouting, fighting, rehearsing, singing and dancing in the classroom itself as well as outside compared to the focus and concentration I witnessed during lesson time. 'These frequent opportunities to relax and engage in vigorous physical activities undoubtedly play an important role in the sustained ability of Japanese children to respond so attentively to their teachers during lessons' (Lee et al, 1995, p162).

Recess also proved to be a time of exploration where children ran freely around the school out of the teachers' sight, enjoying their freedom, a freedom you rarely see entrusted to pupils in England be it due to health and safety concerns and so on . . . Whereas the National Curriculum features heavily in English school life, I felt, in my elementary school that the curriculum was only a fraction of what school was about to the children and teachers. 'Japanese children see school not only as a place to learn, but also a place where they can play and be with their friends. This view is in marked contrast to the stereotype of tense Japanese school children who are so busy with their studies that they have little time for fun' (Lee et al, 1995, pp 162–163).

Consider:

- How does David's experience compare to his experiences in England?
- In terms of curriculum and expectations what might you need to consider for an international placement?

Different learning environments

Each setting that you undertake a placement in will provide a different learning environment, which will in turn have an impact on your teaching and the pupil's learning. There will be classrooms and settings that are extremely well resourced for both the indoors and the outdoors, with adventure playgrounds, nature areas, gardens and vegetable plots. There will be settings that have wonderful displays in every room – with the pupils' work proudly on show for all to see. There will be situations where there is significant adult support – with trained teachers, classroom and learning support assistants and volunteers.

However, you will also find that some schools and settings have very few resources, facilities, amenities or staff to support the pupils, an environment unlike most you will have experienced. There will be many reasons why the situation is as it is – economic, environmental, geographical, historical, social, cultural and religious, and there will be significant factors that you need to take into account when working in such an environment. It may well be a challenge, but in making the most of every situation you will develop as a person and as a professional, and you will gain confidence that you would not have thought possible! Rachel noted that one of the most positive outcomes of her placement in the Gambia was the confidence she gained, and could utilize in her future teaching career.

Case Study: Rachel – Gambia

The classrooms contained very few displays, which had been made by student teachers and there for years, so were faded and damaged. There seemed to be limited interest in displaying the children's work and the few displays they had were not eye catching and did not appear to stimulate the children or interest them.

The Permanent Secretary at the Department of State for Education in the Gambia, Mr. Babucarr Boye (2007) stated that 'In the case of public opinion poll that was carried out on the achievement of learners, the outcome indicated that better learning conditions and output of teachers hinge squarely on the circumstance(s) surrounding them.' If the teachers could provide a positive working environment the children were more likely to want to go to school and learn.

As the school had very few resources lessons were not very interactive and children were not actively involved in their own learning. There were no practical activities and children were expected to copy from the board or a book. The children were given one exercise book for the year and were

Case Study—Cont'd

expected to buy another one if the book was lost or finished, however some children could not afford a second book. Children provided their own pencils, in many cases the children could not afford to buy a pencil and had to share with each other, taking turns to write up their work. Children without an exercise book or without a pencil did not participate in the lesson. Economic circumstances meant that books and materials were scarce and classrooms more so. As Bennett (2007) suggested there seemed to be a huge divide in educational provision between the developed and the developing world.

The children became disinterested and got bored easily. This in turn led to the children misbehaving and disruption of lessons. Some teachers would hit the children, which was a real shock. They said that this was the only way to make the children behave and that hitting the children was part of life in the Gambia. We talked to the tutors with us about this as we were so concerned, and tried to show and explain that we did not hit the children when we taught them.

The use of corporal punishment alarmed the students; it was an aspect of school, family and community life in the Gambia, which they had not expected. The students discussed the issue with tutors and some of the teachers in the school, and said they would not physically punish the children during their lessons. The lack of resources and facilities meant that teaching interesting and interactive lessons was a serious challenge, and that consequently the children and students became distracted and demotivated. The resultant behaviour management issues became a further challenge, exasperated by the normal practice of 'hitting' the children if they misbehaved. Indeed managing the children and students, in a positive, meaningful and respectable way became the major challenge of the placement.

Consider the following questions:

- What would you think if you saw a child/student being hit in your placement school or setting?
- What would you do and/or say, and to whom?
- How can situational and cultural knowledge and understanding help in such an event?

Exploring people and places

One of the most fundamental aspects of a placement is the opportunity it provides to meet new people and visit different places. If your placement is only a short distance from where you live, you will still meet new people and interact with them in a different context. You may have the chance to accompany staff on field trips and visits, and seeing a 'location, place, building' through the eyes of a child is always a learning experience! If you have a more distant placement, then exploring the area and gaining a 'life' experience should be one of your aims and aspirations, as David did!

Case Study: David – Japan

I did lots of travelling while I was there. I spent the odd weekend travelling but also the last two weeks. During my stay I visited Tokyo, Kamakura, Kyoto, Himeji, Hiroshima and Miyajima. I also visited the surrounding area of Nagoya, where certain temples held local celebrations. Most memorable was probably the 'Penis festival' that celebrated fertility. It was very popular with tourists. Another highlight was when I visited the 'Snow festival' in Sapporo. I decided to get the boat which took two days as it was much cheaper than flying as you got a student discount. The only downside to this was that out of the six days I was away, four were spent on a boat.

I am quite adventurous with food and willing to try most things. If anybody wrongly assumes sushi is all that Japanese people eat, they should reconsider this! Japanese cuisine is one of the best I have tried. I ate various dishes, at restaurants, street stalls, home made and at school, where the lunches were excellent. My favourite dish was 'shabu-shabu' a bit like a meat and vegetable hotpot, but you put all the ingredients in at the table. 'Okonomiyaki' are like pancakes topped with cabbage, meat or seafood. 'Takoyaki' are pieces of grilled octopus inside balls of batter. 'Basashi' is raw slices of horse meat, eaten in a similar way to 'sashimi' (raw strips of fish). The most challenging thing I ate was 'natto' which is usually eaten with rice, but they are fermented soya beans that give off a pungent smell. I managed it; it's lucky food isn't a problem for me!

Visiting Japan made me question many values that I take for granted, not just in an educational sense but in a cultural sense as well. The main thing I learnt was that you have to give a lot of time and patience to any new experience you have if you want to get the most out of it. This means going out of your way to make an effort, smiling lots and saying when you don't understand something.

Consider:

- After reflecting on David's case study extract, what might you hope to gain from your placement, in addition to experience working with children and students?
- How can you use these 'experiences' to enhance your personal, professional and academic development?

Socializing and making new friends and colleagues will help to make the placement a 'real' experience. Indeed students have made friendships which survive despite the distance, and make return visits and host visitors. This could also enhance your personal and professional development. However, as with any travel you need to be aware of your own healthy and safety. The penalties for 'inappropriate' behaviour may be far higher in some countries, compared to others. So to make the most of the whole experience, remain aware of customs, beliefs, attitudes, acceptable behaviour, show mutual respect for these and enjoy every situation.

Key points

- Find out as much as you can about your placement – historical, geographical, environmental, economic, social, cultural, religious information as this will have a significant impact on the setting.
- Keep a 'learning journal' as an aide memoir and to reflect and analyse your placement and professional development.
- Make contacts with people that have had previous experience of the placement, setting or location, and seek advice and guidance.
- Your placement may provide the opportunity to experience different beliefs, values, customs and practices, make the most of these and learn from them.
- Make the most of each situation – to get to know new people and places, to explore and try new experiences, to develop knowledge, understanding and skills.
- Be prepared to enjoy every situation – however different or alien it may initially seem, and be willing to share your experiences with others!

Resources

www.britishcouncil.org
www.infed.org/research/keeping_a_journal.htm
www.nationalgeographic.com
www.ofsted.gov.uk
www.reonline.org.uk

5

Look, Listen and Learn

Summary

This chapter will focus on what might be termed the hidden curriculum, with regard to placements. We will be looking at a wide range of factors that affect the success of a placement but are not directly about how you teach children. We will consider how many of these factors relate in some way to relationships and how important it is to begin and develop relationships, with children and adults, thoughtfully and sincerely.

Observation is such an important skill, and is crucial in helping you to understand the way a school or setting functions. We will suggest how careful observation can help you learn important things about your school/setting and class before you begin to prepare for lessons.

We will examine the following areas: presentation of self, observation of staff/children, becoming a colleague, emotional intelligence, settling into your placement and learning environments. As we look at each of these in turn, we will be highlighting the important behaviours expected of you so that the best environment possible is created to successfully enjoy your placement.

Presentation of self

'First impressions count', is a phrase you have probably heard on many occasions. Although there are situations when we change our opinions of people when we get to know them, it is often true that our first impressions do not change much. Placements do not last for long, so that makes it even more important to create a good first impression.

Naumann, Vazire, Rentfrow & Gosling (2009) carried out research to test this hypothesis. It was found that a person's personality is accurately reflected in their appearance.

In the study, observers viewed full-body photographs of 123 people they had never met before. The targets were viewed either in a controlled pose with a neutral facial expression or in a naturally expressed pose. Even when viewing the targets in the controlled pose, the observers could accurately judge some major personality traits, including extraversion and self-esteem. But most traits were hard to detect under these conditions. When observers saw naturally expressive behaviour (such as a smiling expression or energetic stance), their judgments were accurate for nine of the 10 personality traits. The 10 traits were extraversion, agreeableness, conscientiousness, emotional stability, openness, likeability, self-esteem, loneliness, religiosity and political orientation.

'We have long known that people jump to conclusions about others on the basis of very little information,' says Gosling, 'but what's striking about these findings is how many of the impressions have a kernel of truth to them, even on the basis of something as simple a single photograph.'

Gosling cautioned that observers still make plenty of mistakes, but noted that this latest work is important because it sheds new light on the sources of accuracy and inaccuracy of judgments.

With this kind of knowledge, individuals can choose to alter their appearance in specific ways, either to make identity claims or shape others impressions of them, (p8).

In order to ensure you create a good impression, it is helpful to consider what others are expecting from you. Depending on where your placement is, you are likely to meet with the head teacher, your mentor, your class teacher, secretarial staff, support staff, children and students. There may be other adults as well, especially if it is an alternative or international placement. They are all expecting you to be as professional as you can be in your appearance, behaviour and attitudes.

Your appearance is particularly important. If you have done some research before your placement you should know the type of clothes that the staff generally wear and what is socially acceptable. If you have been unable to find out, it is best to err on the side of caution and dress smartly. For example, it may be acceptable to wear jeans to some placements, but many schools do not allow this and would consider it very unprofessional. A track suit would be entirely appropriate for a placement in an Outdoor Education setting; but some schools prefer their staff to only wear sports clothes during PE lessons, and then to change. Whether you agree with the expected dress code in a setting, or not, as a guest you need to be aware of this, or potentially risk creating the impression that you are unprofessional.

Schools and other placement settings sometimes complain when students arrive late and leave early, so ask what time you are expected to arrive and leave before the placement starts, if possible. When transport is provided for you by your placement provider there is a limited amount that you can do about your time of arrival and departure. However, as far as you can, aim to arrive in good time on the first morning and get into good timekeeping habits. This will be noted by the staff you are working with, and commented on positively.

When you arrive at a placement, you may be nervous and perhaps not feel too confident. This can lead you to being perceived as very quiet and reserved, which may not really reflect what you are usually like. Therefore, however you may feel, it is important to make eye contact with whoever is speaking to you and smile. You also need to answer questions with a clear, confident voice and not be afraid to ask if there is something you do not understand. If you are a very confident person by nature, you need to make sure you do not sound overconfident, as this could be perceived as arrogance. Whatever type of placement you are on, you will be expected to show initiative. So on your first day, make sure you ask if there is anything you can do to help. If staff are very busy, look for opportunities to do something useful, rather than waiting to be told what to do.

When you are on an alternative or international placement it is not easy to know exactly what will be expected of you. Dress codes and responsibilities will vary according to the setting that you are in but if you are keen and enthusiastic, arrive in good time and are smartly dressed, this will make a good impression. The preparation recommended in Chapters 3 and 4 is very important. If you have not prepared properly, there is potential for the placement not to be the positive experience you hope it will be.

Observation of staff and children

To be an effective teacher you need to be an effective observer. However, this involves much more than just looking. During early visits to the placement your observations are most likely to be general, so that you gain knowledge and understanding of the placement itself, and the general interactions between the staff and children. The better you understand the context in which you will be working, the more likelihood the placement will be a positive one.

If you are going on an international placement there will be no visit days in advance but there are other ways to find things out such as the buddy system suggested earlier.

Unless you plan to observe particular things, you usually do not remember a lot of what you have seen. Therefore, it is important to have a clear observation focus on your visit days and at the start of your placement. The following questions may help you:

- Do the teachers and other staff appear to enjoy their work?
- How do teachers speak and behave towards each other?
- How do the teachers speak and behave towards the children?
- How do the children speak and behave towards each other?
- How do the children speak and behave towards the teachers and other adults?
- How do the teachers speak and behave towards non-teaching staff?
- How do non-teaching staff speak and behave towards the teachers?
- What do the displays tell you about how the school environment is valued?
- What do the displays tell you about how children's work is valued?
- Is the school welcoming for parents?

It is easy not to notice some of these things unless you are carefully observing them. However, they should give you a good idea of the ethos of the school or setting and what things are valued. We will investigate observations later in this chapter.

Emotional intelligence

It is important to remember that just as you are observing others, other people are observing you. Therefore, how you respond to the new situations you are facing will have a huge impact on the success of your placement. The term emotional intelligence covers all kinds of skills that are important in forming good relationships with others and being accepted as a team member. Teachers need these skills and qualities.

In 1995 emotional intelligence came to public attention as a result of a book by Daniel Goleman 'Emotional intelligence: why it can matter more than IQ'. Goleman himself, in association with the Hay Group, developed the following model of competencies:

1. Personal competence: these competencies determine how we manage ourselves.
   Self-awareness: knowing one's internal states, preferences, resources and intuitions.
   Emotional self-awareness: recognizing one's emotions and their effects.

Accurate self-assessment: knowing one's strengths and limits.

Self-confidence: a strong sense of one's self-worth and capabilities.

Self-management: managing one's internal states, impulses and resources.

Self-control: keeping disruptive emotions and impulses in check.

Trustworthiness: maintaining standards of honesty and integrity.

Conscientiousness: taking responsibility for personal performance.

Adaptability: flexibility in handling change.

Achievement-orientation: striving to improve or meeting a standard of excellence.

Initiative: readiness to act on opportunities.

2. Social competence: these competencies determine how we handle relationships.

Social awareness: awareness of others' feelings, needs and concerns.

Empathy: sensing others' feelings and perspectives, and taking an active interest in their concerns.

Organizational awareness: reading a group's emotional currents and power relationships.

Service orientation: anticipating, recognizing and meeting customers' needs.

Social skills: adeptness at inducing desirable responses in others.

Developing others: sensing others' developmental needs and bolstering their abilities.

Leadership: inspiring and guiding individuals and groups

Influence: wielding effective tactics for persuasion.

Communication: listening openly and sending convincing messages.

Change catalyst: initiating or managing change.

Conflict management: negotiating and resolving disagreements.

Building bonds: nurturing instrumental relationships.

Teamwork and collaboration: working with others toward shared goals. Creating group synergy in pursuing collective goals.

www.cipd.co.uk/subjects/lrnanddev/selfdev/emotintel.htm

When you look at this list initially you may consider it to be huge. However, these skills and qualities are ones that you should seek to develop. They will help you to be sensitive to situations and respond appropriately. Consider the following examples:

Example 1: Social Awareness

Imagine that you arrive at your placement on the first morning, and you notice that your teacher looks as though she has been crying. There are a lot of things that you need to find out from her. If you are simply focused on your own needs you will go straight to her and ask for the kinds of information you need. However, if you are sensitive to this situation you will ask politely if there is a suitable time during the day when you could talk with her. Your cautious and sensitive approach will help in forming a good relationship.

Example 2: Trustworthiness

You have had a difficult weekend due to the illness of a friend or family member. As a result you haven't done all the planning you should have done and some of the children's work has not been marked. You can pretend that you have done everything, hope that your teacher will not notice and try to catch up on Monday night. Alternatively, you can explain to your teacher exactly what has happened. If you lie and your teacher finds out, you will have lost her trust and gained a reputation for being dishonest. Honesty and integrity are very important qualities in a teacher and should always be maintained.

Example 3: Teamwork and collaboration

You are in a two form entry school. The parallel classes follow the same curriculum, and you are asked to plan certain lessons that will be taught in both classes. Once you have planned the lesson, you need to gather together a number of resources. You do not have much time, so it would be much easier to get your own resources and leave the other teacher to get his/her own. However, you know it would not really be a lot of work for you to do two copies of everything you need. If you choose the first option, you will save yourself a few minutes, but in so doing you will show that you are not good as a member of a team. By making the extra effort, you will be recognized as a helpful team member.

Example 4: Initiative

Case Study: Carolyn – Art Gallery

After initially observing and examining what the gallery already had in place, I began to see the potential for using my own teaching expertise to adapt some of the existing workshops. I planned my own re-vamped sessions using the same resources in different ways. I gained the permission of the education officer to deliver these re-vamped sessions to visiting school groups. The first session I planned and delivered was called the Portraits session, aimed at a group of Key Stage 1 children.

It would have been much easier for Carolyn to do what she was asked and no more. However, she wanted to make the most of her placement and by using her initiative she opened up new possibilities and her placement was hugely successful.

Example 5: Conscientiousness/Achievement-orientation

You are on your final block placement and everything is going fairly well. Your mentor is pleased with you but points out there are several areas where you can improve if you really work hard. In this situation some students decide to coast along to the end of their placement, knowing they will pass. You can choose to do this and your workload will be easier but those trying to help you will be disappointed in you and you will miss out on the opportunity to improve as much as you can before you begin your teaching career. No doubt the quality of the reference you receive from that school will reflect their opinion of your lack of effort.

Becoming a colleague

It is one thing to be a student on a placement and a completely different thing to become accepted as a colleague. However, when a placement goes really well, this is what happens and it is not by accident. There are many things you can do to help this to happen and also some things that, if you do them, will ensure it will not happen.

One of the most important aspects that you need to consider is to recognize and acknowledge that you are a guest in the school. This means that you need to be polite and appreciative in your communications with the staff and the children. There may be times when you consider that you are not receiving the support you need or you have some other issue. It is particularly at these times that you need to be professional. Even if you are tempted you should try not to be abrupt or rude, as this will immediately ensure you will not be accepted as a colleague in that school or setting.

On any placement there are certain things you are entitled to, in terms of observations and guidance from your class teacher and mentor or supervisor. However, you also have responsibilities such as being punctual, doing the planning and preparation and listening to advice. The important point is to keep these things in balance. If you do all the things expected of you, and show enthusiasm doing them, then it is more likely that the placement staff will be willing to do the things expected of them.

In order to be accepted as a colleague, one of the important things to learn is staff room etiquette and how to read hidden messages or rules. Staff rooms are very important places for teachers and all staff members, where they can have a few minutes of relaxation away from the hurly-burly of the classroom. They may only be in there a very short amount of time in the day so those few minutes are very precious. You may find that there are expectations of behaviour in every staffroom and it is vital that you discover what is and what is not acceptable.

There may be a procedure for tea and coffee. Find out how much you are expected to pay and make sure that you do so promptly. You need to know if there are spare mugs. It may be useful to take your own mug as you can cause unintended offence by using a teacher's prize possession without permission!

Sometimes certain teachers bring their own coffee or tea bags for a particular reason so make sure you ask before making yourself a drink, out of professional courtesy. These may sound very trivial, but small issues can lead to further issues, and hinder successful professional relationships.

In some staffrooms teachers have particular chairs where they always sit so again, make sure you ask if it is all right to sit anywhere. Once you know how to get a drink and where to sit there are other factors you should keep in mind. Often there are conversations in staffrooms about children and parents and sometimes regarding other staff members. Remember, these conversations are confidential. Teachers sometimes say things in the heat of the moment when they have just come from a stressful lesson. Anything you hear should not be repeated outside of the staff room, or you could find yourself in a potentially awkward situation.

Case Study

Student A was on a placement and formed negative views about the school and its resources. She did not keep these views to herself and was overheard at lunch time, while waiting in the local shop for a sandwich, complaining to a friend about the school. Unfortunately for her, another member of staff was also in the shop at the time and reported the conversation to the head teacher. Needless to say news about this spread quickly throughout the staff and student A had no chance of being accepted as a colleague. She was fortunate that the head teacher allowed her to complete her placement. You need to be aware of what is accepted behaviour in the staffroom.

Case Study

Student B caused offence in his school by swearing. This upset several members of staff, and his training provider was informed when the swearing happened on the second occasion. He was given a warning by his tutor not to swear in the staffroom but he did not heed the warning, and on the next occasion the school asked him to leave. He only had himself to blame, and if he had behaved responsibly, the school would have been happy to support him.

Case Study

Student C caused concern in a staff room by spending almost all of her time, using her mobile phone. She was not at all sociable and everyone else had to listen to her conversations. They felt strongly that she was abusing the privilege of being allowed in the staff room. If you need to make a telephone call at lunchtime, go somewhere private to do so. With all of these potential problems, you might think it would be safer not to go into the staffroom but that is certainly not the answer.

Case Study

Student D was shy and felt uncomfortable going into the staff room. She decided it was easier to eat her lunch in the classroom and spend the rest of the time preparing for the next lesson. When asked by her teacher, she said she had a lot of things to get ready. Other teachers noticed and it was reported to her University tutor. The tutor spoke with Student D and pointed out that one section of the QTS Standards is about 'Communicating and working with others'. It is impossible to meet those Standards if you isolate yourself from colleagues. In most schools or settings, teachers expect you to go into the staffroom and to be sociable. They will be happy for you to be there as long as you use your common sense and behave appropriately.

Teaching is not just about what happens between 9 a.m. and 3 p.m. in the classroom. Teachers expect you to realize this and you may want to volunteer to go out on playground duty and to help with extracurricular activities, if it is at all possible. If transport is provided and you cannot stay very late, find out if there are any clubs held at lunch time that you could assist with. Find out if it is appropriate to you to stay for staff meetings. There may be occasions when there is some staff development and you should join in, if it is possible.

There are often parents' evenings, school plays or school fairs that occur while you are on placement in a school. Although attendance at these will not be part of your placement requirements, it will be very much appreciated by the staff if you make an effort to be there, and you could reference this to the TDA (2008) QTS Standards. Teachers have to give up their time for these kinds of events, and if you do the same it will be noticed, as well as giving you a valuable insight into extra curricular activities in the setting.

In summary, being accepted as a colleague comes down to giving and receiving. If you give wholehearted effort on your placement in every aspect, you will deserve, and usually receive, the respect of the staff you work with, and the acceptance that you hope for.

Settling into your placement

In Chapters 3 and 4 we discussed a wide range of aspects you should consider in preparation for a placement and these will give you some knowledge of the context in which you will be working. We are going to focus now on developing that knowledge as soon as your placement commences. We have already discussed some factors you should look out for but the importance of observing carefully cannot be overestimated. If you have not been able to look at the policies of your school or setting in advance, you should look at the key policies as soon as you can. Particularly, you should read the behaviour management policy and the health and safety policy. It is also very useful to read the prospectus for parents, and sometimes schools have guidance notes especially for students.

The earlier you understand the routines of your school or setting the better. Observe carefully and ask questions if you are not sure what is expected of you. For example, when teachers arrive in the morning, do they spend time in the staffroom or go straight to the classroom?

Case Study

Student D arrived at her school at just after 8 a.m. every morning, which was very commendable. However, she went straight to the staffroom and sat drinking coffee for most of the time before school started which was not at all the routine of the staff, and was not received well.

There are other routines that teachers have which you must learn. The following questions will help you:

- What do teachers do when the bell goes at the start of school? Watch carefully the procedure for bringing children into the classroom.
- Do teachers stay in the hall for collective worship?
- If not, are they expected to do anything particular?
- What is the procedure at break times and lunchtimes?

There are a lot of other aspects that you can focus on when you are observing in the classroom or the place where you will be working. This will help you when you get to the stage of planning which will be discussed in Chapter 6. Some of the key aspects that you should look out for include:

- Organization of room and resources: Take note of the layout of the room, how the tables and chairs are arranged. Look carefully where resources are stored. Is there a carpet area? Where is the whiteboard situated? Is there a sink for art activities? How many display boards are there? The answers to each of these questions will help you when you start your planning.
- Class/year group/ability/number of children: Your teacher will probably provide you with a class list and details of the abilities of the children. It is worth finding out about how the children are grouped and whether any of the children have special educational needs. On an alternative placement it may be a different group of children each day so you may not be able to discover much information in advance
- Behaviour management strategies: whatever type of placement you are on, behaviour management will be an issue. Watch carefully how the teachers gain attention. Children like routines so it is always a good idea to continue the routines they are used to. This will be discussed in more detail in Chapter 6.
- Rewards and sanctions: notice how the teacher uses rewards and sanctions; and positive reinforcement.
- Roles of other adults: notice how many other adults are involved working with your class and what their roles are.
- Introductions: your teacher will probably have a normal routine for introducing lessons.
- Transitions: be aware of how transitions from one activity to another are managed.
- Conclusions/Plenary: just as with the introduction to lessons, your teacher probably has a routine for concluding lessons. This will not just be about tidying up, even though that it is very important. It will also be about reviewing the learning.

If you are required to develop your own system for observations, then it may be useful to keep a journal. Each visit could be recorded in the journal, to include general and focused observation notes, which could then be highlighted, analysed and used for your planning, teaching and learning.

Active listening

We have discussed observation in some detail, but it is also necessary to consider active listening. A fundamental determinant of any placement is the ability to listen and to respond accordingly. Whether this is listening to a child when they say they need to go to the toilet, or listening to a teacher when they say that unless you improve the content of your lesson/activity plans you will be unlikely to be successful in the placement. Teachers and practitioners are normally very effective 'talkers', but may find it more difficult to 'listen'. Sometimes this is due to time pressures, when too many other things need to be done to have time to listen properly; or it is too stressful to listen intently at the end of a long and challenging day. Another plausible reason is the necessity 'to get through the content' as speedily as possible, to get on to the next area. However, being able to listen, demonstrates you are listening, taking on board and acting on guidance you have been given. This is often a key to achieving a successful placement.

Learning environment

In this chapter, we have considered many of the issues that make up the learning environment. It is created by the relationships within the school or setting, and by its ethos. Learning environments are situation specific. However much you find out about a school or setting in advance, it is only when you get there that you truly experience what the place is like. For example, sometimes it is possible to reach uninformed conclusions based on the wealth of resources available or the lack of resources, and although these may be an indicator of the catchment area they are no guarantee that the learning environment is good. There are some international placement and alternative placement opportunities where there will be very few resources, and yet there is an effective environment based on relationships and attitudes towards learning.

By learning as much as you can through careful observation, and by using your emotional intelligence to form good relationships with staff and children, you will give yourself the best possible chance for your placement to be enjoyable and successful. Having this recorded in the form of a journal will also provide a useful tool to aid you with reflections and evaluations, and to critically analyse situations.

Key points

- Make a good first impression by being punctual, appropriately dressed and enthusiastic.
- Observe carefully and learn as much as you can about the routines and practices.
- Be aware and sensitive to situations and respond appropriately.

- You are a guest in the school or setting, so find out about and respect staffroom or shared area practice.
- Actively listen and act upon advice you are given.

Resources

http://eqi.org/steps.htm (this site is about basic steps to emotional intelligence in the classroom)

www.teachers.tv/videos/teaching-practice

6

Getting the Basics Right

Summary

The initial excitement about going on a placement may be slightly affected by the mention of planning, preparing resources, behaviour management, assessment, learning and teaching and the curriculum! However, these are integral to success, and if you manage to get these 'basics' right, the more likely you are to have a positive and hopefully meaningful, memorable and perhaps life enhancing experience. In the following chapter we detail some aspects of the 'basics', which could act as a guide during your preparation. We include a range of case study extracts under each section, to illustrate the points being made, in action. It is well intentioned to say 'plan well, get your resources ready and make sure you assess' but the reality of the placement situation may make this appear less than straight forward. Hence, the inclusion of case study extracts so that you can hear the 'voices' of those that have undertaken a diverse range of placements – all positive, meaningful, memorable and life enhancing experiences.

Curriculum

In order to ensure that learning and teaching is effective and appropriate you will need to consider the curriculum or guidelines that you will need to work to. You have your own Standards to achieve to gain Qualified Teacher Status (QTS) and the placement will support your achievement of many aspects of this, which you will need to keep a record of. However the actual curriculum that serves as a basis for your planning may be different for each placement. If you are on a traditional placement you will be using the National Curriculum or the Early Years Foundation Stage Framework but this may be different for an alternative placement and probably will be different on an international placement. You need to establish, as soon as you know where your placement will be, which curriculum or guidelines you will be expected to use, and to ask for copies, if available.

Planning

Irrespective of whether you are on a traditional placement, with a whole school experience file, or two, to develop; or on an alternative or international placement, you will be expected to plan appropriately. Your training provider will supply planning proformas; lesson/activity plan templates, guidance and examples, and you should use these where possible. However, your placement setting may have alternative planning documents and processes in which case you may be expected to adopt these. If these are significantly different from those provided by your training provider you should discuss this with a tutor, to ensure that what you are doing will meet expectations and requirements.

In Chapter 3, we discussed the importance of preparation before your placement begins. On your first visit days, you need to find out as much as you can about the children you will be teaching and the subject areas and topics. This will help you ensure your planning is appropriate to the children you will be teaching. Once your teaching begins, it is vital that you evaluate lessons. Whether or not you are asked to write an evaluation of every lesson it is important that you think through what happened, as this should inform your future planning.

Consider the following questions:

- Were the learning outcomes appropriate?
- Was there sufficient differentiation?
- Were the resources appropriate?
- Did you allow enough time for the different parts of the lesson?
- Did the children and students gain new knowledge and understanding, or develop a skill, as a result of your planned lesson?
- Did the children enjoy the lesson?
- Did the children achieve the learning outcomes?

As your placement progresses there will be further planning on a daily and weekly basis and you always need to be ready to change aspects in response to your lesson evaluations.

In the following case studies you will see the importance of communication with your teacher and other staff throughout the planning process. David undertook a traditional placement in a Foundation Unit of a Primary school. He had worked in nurseries before starting his teacher training, and had undertaken a placement in a KS1 class during his first year of training. He noted that each school and setting had its own way of planning and that it was necessary to become as familiar with this as possible, before the placement started.

Case Study: David – Traditional

The planning process began every Wednesday during PPA time. We would discuss the topic (if new), areas already covered, areas to be covered and activities that would be suitable. Planning was done as a team, with everybody providing some input and several focus activities were planned for the week. The main focus and independent activities were fed back to the teaching assistants for them to adapt and add their ideas. The teaching assistants then helped to plan for the outdoor activities, as well as the table top activities that would be rotated every two days for two weeks.

All teachers and teaching assistants were very supportive of each other's ideas but also realistic. Often we had a wealth of activities that we could not cover in the proposed week. Once I had been allocated or suggested an activity, I would go away and plan this in further detail. For the activity I would plan an introduction, main and plenary. Sometimes the introduction and plenary was a whole group or whole class process. I would differentiate to three levels, including an SEN section as appropriate. If support staff were involved I would detail what they would be doing and explain this to them before the lesson. For the activity I was expected to cover all sixty children so this would usually take me three days, but sometimes four, to teach. I worked with around six children in a group and after each group I would annotate the activity plan to show different ideas or approaches that evolved during the activity.

Consider:

- What are some of the key factors in planning as part of a team?
- How did David seek to address the needs of all the children?

Sally was both excited and apprehensive about the challenges of planning on her alternative placement in a Special school. By taking on board suggestions made by tutors and staff at the school she gained a very positive experience.

Case Study: Sally – Special school

Planning within the Special setting was quite scary at first! I felt over-whelmed by the amount of things I had to consider when planning, including the children's Individual Education Plan (IEP) targets, the Pivot or National Curriculum Level they were working at, advice and recommendations from outside agencies such as educational psychologists, physiotherapists, speech and language therapists, the topic being covered within the school at the time and the children's very varied ages and interests.

Prior to planning any activities for the children I decided it was important to meet them and develop an understanding of their specific interests. Although there were significantly fewer children in this setting than in previous mainstream classes I had taught the interests were much more diverse, possibly on account of the range of ages present.

Throughout the placement I was supported by all of the staff. Many of the children's key workers took the time to tell me more about their individual children and some of the teachers discussed things they had tried in the past when covering the same/similar objectives to me. The staff really helped me to consider my objectives and the learning steps I was expecting the children to make, they encouraged me to take one objective and break it down to list all of the things you had to be able to do in order to achieve it.

This was quite an eye opening experience as it made me realise that often there are many small parts to achieving one learning objective. While it was important to have realistic expectations and to ensure that the learning objectives were attainable it was also important that we continued to have high expectations and to challenge the children. Having been through the process of breaking down the learning objective it enabled me to see that although all of the pupils may not always have achieved the end goal they had often made progress towards it which, instead of celebrating, I would have previously overlooked.

Consider:

- How could the learning objective 'to be able to retell a story' be broken down into 'smaller steps'?
- Can you make a list of all the things a child or student would need to be able to do, before they could achieve this objective?

Resources

An essential part of good planning is deciding and preparing the resources that you will use. You may expect that all the resources you need during a traditional school experience will be provided for you by the school. However, this may not be the case. Most schools will expect that you will ask for, and be able to use some of the resources they have available but they may also expect you to make or bring in some resources of your own. These need not necessarily be expensive resources that you have bought specifically for the experience; but could be resources you have loaned from your training provider library or donated to you by family and friends keen to support you in your teacher training. David's experience again highlights the importance of speaking with your teacher.

Case Study: David – Traditional

The school had a wide range of resources that were readily accessible. I found that a key part of the planning was to discuss what resources were available. Although this may seem quite basic, planning as a group gave all people the chance to share their ideas, as well as knowledge of the available resources. This proved especially key in locating the resources! The most valuable resource, however, was the ratio of adults to children. This enabled staff to work with smaller groups of children for either support or extension activities.

Consider:

- How will you find out what resources are available in a particular school or setting?
- More specifically, how would you confirm which resources are available for you to use, and which may not be?

Hopefully, you will begin to develop a resource bank of your own, as this will prove extremely useful and beneficial during your placement and in your teaching career. A basic resource pack could include:

- Pens, pencils, crayons, felt pens, erasers, sharpeners, scissors (left and right handed), hole punch, stapler, sellotape, glue, coloured paper and card, coloured felt.

Additional resources that could usefully be collected to develop a resource bank include:

- Children's Fictional Books suitable for different ages and reading ability
- Children's Information and Factual Books for different ages and reading ability
- Teacher's Tips books – such as 'displays', 'creative activities', 'templates' etc.
- Historical stories and artefacts
- Maps and globes

- Pictures, posters, prints
- Maths based resources – number cards, number fans, dice and counting games
- Board games – such as Snakes and Ladders
- Cards – lotto, snap, happy families etc.
- Jigsaws – for different ages and ability
- Story Sacks
- Outdoor resources – balls, bats, skittles, skipping ropes etc.

All of these resources will prove useful for any traditional or alternative placement. However, greater thought is needed to be given if you are preparing to go on an international placement, not least because of the issue of luggage weight and customs regulations and guidelines, as detailed in Chapter 3.

Depending on your destination, and the actual placement, you may want to take resources for the children and/or school. If you know from your preparatory research, discussions with tutors and students/teachers that have visited before, that the school or setting you are visiting has very few resources, you may want to take some. However you need to think carefully about the most useful resources, for you and for the children and setting. Taking many bars of chocolate may initially be a good idea but, will you be able to take these through customs? What happens if they all melt? Would there be anywhere to cool them? Would there be health and safety issues? Would this fit with the school or setting's healthy eating programme – if they have one?

Resources to take abroad

Tutors are often asked 'what should I take with me?' when preparing for an international placement. This obviously depends on the country, location and setting you will be working in, and the facilities and services there may be. The following is an indicative list of some of the items you could consider taking with you.

- Appropriate clothing, depending on the weather, climate, conditions, and nature of the placement, which could include:
- Fabric walking boots
- Light clothing (including some with long sleeves as evenings may be cool/cold and insects prevalent)
- Warm clothing (including snow wear), if appropriate
- Waterproof clothing
- Clothes for working in a school or setting
- Casual wear
- Towel and swim wear, as appropriate

- Teaching resources – paper, crayons, pencils, laminated work and pictures, for display or to use as a stimulus
- Journal/notebook and pens
- Deet insect repellent/insect bite cream/spray
- Anti-malarial tablets (as appropriate)
- Sufficient medication (that you normally take)
- Painkillers
- Stomach upset medication
- Basic first aid kit – plasters, bandage, wipes, antiseptic cream etc.
- High factor sun screen/ sun block/ lip sun block/salve
- Sun hat/ sunglasses
- Wet wipes and wash kit
- Toothbrush, toothpaste etc.
- Camera
- Water bottle
- Money/travellers cheques (keep a separate record of numbers)
- Passport and visa (if required)
- Inoculation record
- Proof and details of holiday insurance cover

Sally, despite her initial reservations, found that many of the resources from traditional school placements were useful and appropriate in a Special school.

Case Study: Sally – Special school

Once I understood the content my lessons were to have I started to formulate ideas for activities and collect resources. Many of the resources were available from the school although some were borrowed from other local 'Special Settings' and, much to my surprise, from mainstream environments. This was an interesting discovery as previously I had viewed 'Special Settings' in isolation and perceived there would be very few similarities between them and mainstream settings. Subsequently I realised that there was actually much common ground between the educational settings and as such mutually beneficial relationships could be formed.

During my time at the Unit I also realised that many things could constitute resources and work well without being expensive or specialised. This was a revelation and made me realise that the pupils I was teaching, despite the diagnostic labels, were essentially just like any other set of children I had taught.

Consider:

- Can you produce a list of resources that would be useful for you when you are preparing for a placement?
- Are there resources that you already have that you could utilize on your placement?

Behaviour management

The most overwhelming concern that students always cite prior to any placement is behaviour management. 'What if the children don't listen to what I say or ask them to do? What will I do if the children behave inappropriately'? This can become even more of a challenge if the children do not speak English, and you do not speak their home language, or the children have been diagnosed with severe behavioural issues. However, lots of support is available and there is much you can learn.

The following advice is to help you avoid some common errors that it is possible to make on any kind of educational placement:

- Interesting lessons promote good behaviour. If you plan and prepare well so that children are motivated to learn you will significantly reduce inappropriate behaviour.
- Be aware of the school and class policy. Find out what rewards and sanctions are used by the teacher. At first, it is good to follow normal practice. Always speak to your teacher before you introduce any new system.
- Try not to be too friendly. You are a teacher and not there to become a friend of the children. Children will ask personal questions but you should avoid answering them. If you are a good teacher children will like you, so concentrate on being a good teacher.
- Sound as though you mean what you say. If you speak in a timid voice when you are asking children to be quiet or to do a particular task, the children may not respond. You need to sound authoritative even if your knees are knocking!
- Make sure children are listening to you. If you have asked children to be quiet, wait until they are quiet before continuing.
- Use praise when children behave well. It is often better to praise the children who are doing what you asked. Remember the importance of positive reinforcement – praising what is done well, rather than focussing on what is wrong.

In every placement you undertake there will be experienced staff who will be able to guide and support you. Try to observe teachers and other adults and the strategies they use and discuss potential concerns. Your training provider will also be able to advise you, if necessary, so ask if you need to. Before David's placement in a Foundation Stage Unit, he was not overly concerned with behaviour management issues, but recognized that each setting has different expectations and policies. The more that he was able to find out about behaviour management in the setting, the better.

Case Study: David – Traditional

Generally the children were very well behaved although, as can be expected, there were times when certain procedures had to be followed. As I was working in a Unit, the response and expectations of all staff had to be constant. There was a 'time out' chair that was used on the third warning. Children would be asked to think about a question given to them by the teacher. Once they were ready to participate appropriately they could rejoin the group/activity. Afterwards the teacher would ask about their response to the question. This worked very well and was very effective with the majority of the children.

When dealing with any issues I learnt to remain calm but assertive. I often asked the children to talk through what had happened and what did they think I should do. This was a useful way to encourage the children to take responsibility for their own actions. It generally worked well unless a child refused to admit the truth; this then led to consideration of 'telling the truth', and the perception of this for a five year old.

Consider:

- What types of behaviour management strategies could you use on your placement?
- Are there strategies that might be more appropriate in certain settings or situations, compared to others?

Carolyn was concerned that the 'openness' and lack of traditional structure of the school day would mean that behaviour management would be a major issue, during her alternative placement in an Art Gallery. However her initial fears were soon dispelled as she realized that effective teaching and behaviour management strategies can be transferred to any setting.

Case Study: Carolyn – Art Gallery

I quickly realised that the gallery itself was a key player in managing behaviour. The surroundings so captured the children's interest that they rarely misbehaved at all. In the workshop, free from the confines and restrictions that a classroom desk and chair normally place on a child, they were able to fully engage in the activities. Children appeared to enjoy being able to sprawl out in a space to paint, draw or sculpt in a way that was more comfortable for them, rather than being stuck in the more formal sitting

Case Study—Cont'd

position. The most important thing I learnt about behaviour management during my time at the gallery is that a child who feels both comfortable and interested in the task they are doing does not tend to misbehave. Accompanying teachers often commented how a child who usually misbehaved in school had been surprisingly well-behaved, focused and on task during their trip to the gallery. To me, this confirms that making children comfortable and interested in what they are doing is a superb strategy for managing behaviour.

Consider:

- Why do you think that Carolyn had few behaviour management issues during her placement?
- Could you apply these factors to other settings and situations?

Adelle's experience in America also illustrates how the environment can be an important factor in children's behaviour.

Case Study: Adelle – America

During my time in both schools in Holland, Michigan the behaviour of the children was excellent. When talking with other students out there on placement the consensus of opinion was one that the majority of the children in school were very well behaved. Through observations there were many factors that contributed to this. The classroom sizes were huge; the children all had plenty of space to work and so weren't cramped on top of each other. The classes were very structured and although lacked the much needed creativity they did give the children a sense of routine and the children were able to expect what was coming next in their curriculum.

The children were also allowed to be children outside on the playground and were given the most fabulous resources I have ever seen in a school playground. Jungle gyms and swing sets as far as the eye could see; the outdoor area was immense. What was refreshing to see was that the children were swinging and jumping without a worried teacher flinching as each child moved, just in case they fell. This enabled the children to really let off steam and challenge their bodies physically when on their playtime. In turn the children came back into class ready to sit down and focus on the task. The staff and children offered each other lots of praise and were proud to highlight their achievements; in turn this contributed to the children's

Case Study—Cont'd

feeling of self worth and so affected their behaviour in a positive way. Through these observations the most important thing I learnt from my time in America was that to gain good behaviour you need to provide the children with structure and challenge, both in the classroom and outside.

Consider:

- Why do you think that Adelle had few behaviour management issues during her placement?
- Could you apply these factors to other settings and situations?

Learning and teaching

The intention of any placement is to give you the opportunity to gain experience and to enhance your teaching and the children's learning. If you focus, and re-focus on this during the preparation stage and the placement itself, it will help you to keep a realistic perspective. There have been many attempts to define different learning styles, which you can usefully research. However, at a basic level you need to be imaginative and provide lessons and activities that stimulate and motivate the children.

On any placement you need to ensure that the entire focus is not just on the activities that the children will undertake. It is great if they are highly motivated by the activities, but essentially, the most important aspect is that the children are learning. You need to have a focus on what the children will learn, and then concentrate on the activities, rather than the other way round.

Being able to reflect on your teaching and the children's learning, and to critically analyse what worked well and what did not, why this was the case and how it could be improved, are fundamental skills. One of the most significant reasons the case study students had such positive placements was their ability to critically reflect and analyse, and to act on this to enhance their practice. They were also able to articulate how this informed future practice. We will return to a case study extract included in Chapter 2 but concentrate on how Carolyn reflected and analysed her lessons in order to improve the learning experience for the children.

Case Study: Carolyn – Art Gallery

After initially observing and examining what the gallery already had in place, I began to see the potential for using my own teaching expertise to adapt some of the existing workshops. I planned my own re-vamped sessions using the same resources in different ways. I gained the permission of the education officer to deliver these re-vamped sessions to visiting school groups. The first session I planned and delivered was called the Portraits session, aimed at a group of Key Stage 1 children.

The main learning objective for the session was to understand how artists reproduce the face in portrait work. The session was based around the visual stimulus of a sculpture and paintings of portraits displayed in the gallery. First the children would look closely at portrait work produced by artists before having a go at sketching and copying some of the facial features they could see in the artists' work. The children then went into the workshop area where they worked in small groups using their sense of touch to physically explore the size and orientation of their own faces.

This practical approach really helped the children to understand the relative size of facial features in comparison to one another. After exploring their faces kinaesthetically, I then directed the children to create self portraits out of clay. The previous activity meant they could use their finger-thumb measurements of their facial features to get more accurate size and orientation in their clay work. The results were very successful and the children went away with a much broader understanding of portrait work than when they arrived.

Soon after the success of adapting and delivering the Portraits session, a local school contacted the gallery enquiring if they had a workshop suitable for their Year 2 class, focused on the topic 'People Who Help Us' which they were studying in school. At the time the gallery didn't have any such workshops so I volunteered to do a new session which would be more suitable.

Again I focused the session on a visual resource already present in the gallery – a huge landscape painting of Lake Windermere by eighteenth century artist Philippe Jacques De Loutherbourg. The painting is titled 'Windermere in a storm' as it depicts a stormy Lake Windermere with a small boat and it's passengers in trouble. The painting shows some figures reaching out to help the passengers to safety. I entitled the session 'Helping Hands' and prompted a discussion with the children about people who might help in such a situation as depicted in the painting. Afterwards the children went to the workshop area where they could choose from a variety of practical, cross-curricular activities relating to the topic Helping Hands. The practical activities covered a range of National Curriculum objectives relating to different subjects including; literacy (speaking, listening and drama), art (painting, drawing, colour), PSHE (working together) and science (light using the light box and projector). This shows how a single painting can be used to promote a variety of learning experiences across the curriculum.

Consider:

- How did Carolyn's reflection and analysis help to prepare further lessons and activities?
- What impact did this have on learning and teaching?

Assessment and record keeping

After 'behaviour management', 'assessment' is often the most dreaded word during a placement. 'Have you done any assessment yet?' 'Where is your assessment file?' 'What are your assessments telling you about the children's learning?' Assessment is an integral part of the learning and teaching cycle and needs to be planned for. However, in practice, little seems to be mentioned about assessment until the placement is well underway, and then uncertainty may set in as you think you haven't done any! You will have been assessing the children from your first observations, but keeping records of this and using the assessments to inform future planning and practice may be a different matter!

As with most aspects of learning and teaching, preparation is the key to effective assessment. Try to find out the assessment that is undertaken in the school or setting, and what the expectations will be with regard to assessment during the placement. When you first begin your training you will not be expected to do much assessment and record-keeping. However, as you progress, the requirements will become greater. You can save time by constructing templates on which to record your assessment results before your placement begins. On your lesson plans it is helpful to have a section where you include how you will assess the learning from that lesson. When the lesson produces an end product assessment can take place later, but there are times when you want to assess the process, not just the product. On those occasions assessment may be by observation or by discussion with the child to find out what they have learned. Assessment will often be formative and not necessarily recorded, but you do need to ensure you have a system for regularly recording assessment results. In the following case study extract, Sally outlines one such approach.

Case Study: Sally – Special school

During this placement I was expected to assess and record formatively and set targets for pupil learning. Assessment would occur against the learning objectives of the sessions, which often included IEP targets, speech and language therapy targets and other more 'holistic' targets, alongside the more traditional 'academic' targets. The deeper understanding of progression I had developed from breaking down the learning objectives for planning purposes had a huge an impact on the way I undertook this assessment. I found that 'objective achieved' or 'not achieved' was no longer sufficient. Instead I found that I was writing more about what the pupils' did and

Case Study—Cont'd

looking for the small steps. Although this was beneficial it was hard to see at a glance where the children were. A member of staff suggested high-lighting the children's names on my assessment sheet – green for achieved and exceeded objective, yellow for objective achieved and red for objective not achieved – this gave it immediate visual impact but I also had the smaller steps that children had achieved noted down too.

Before commencing this placement pupils' written work had always formed much of my assessment evidence. However, for some children in this setting, and with hindsight for some children I have taught in mainstream settings, this was not a fair reflection of their progress nor did it sit well with the more practical approach to learning I tried to implement. As such I was a little unsure how I was going to provide evidence of the children's learning. I approached the staff at the unit about it and they were fantastic. They encour-aged me to take photographs of the children undertaking the activities, print them off, write the date and the learning objective on them and place them in the pupil's file. Originally I was a little sceptical about my photographic skills and my ability to get round all of the children with the camera and thus the standard of evidence I was collecting but with the support of the other adults in the classroom this method worked really well. The evidence collected also provided something for the children and parents to look at, at a later date.

I have since applied all of these techniques to my teaching in mainstream and have definitely found assessment easier to manage as a result. Assess-ment does not have to mean copious amounts of paper work; it is about finding a method that works for you in your setting.

Consider:

- How did Sally collect evidence of the children's and student's learning?
- How did she use this evidence to inform her planning and practice?

An alternative placement can be extremely useful for developing forms of assessment, and for encouraging you to be more creative and innovative. In the following case study Carolyn explains how her ideas developed.

Case Study: Carolyn – Art Gallery

Assessment was an element of the placement that I wasn't initially sure how to handle. I was used to assessing children on paper with numbers, percent-ages and levels. The art gallery didn't really have a place for this kind of assessment. Through observing and participating in workshops I realised

Case Study—Cont'd

that assessment still played a big part in the learning experiences of the children, it just took a less formal form. Questioning and discussion were used to a great extent within the gallery itself. In particular, the use of open questions about pieces of artwork enabled children to give differentiated responses.

It was clear through listening to children's responses that there were a range of levels in their observation, analytical and reflective skills. Open questions allowed children to answer and perform at an appropriate level for them as individuals, while also remaining accessible to all abilities. During practical activities, it was easy to assess children through observation – such as assessing the level of their fine motor control, grasp of colour or sculpting techniques. As the children were always engaged in practical activities it meant there was always a tangible outcome which also helped in terms of assessment. If anything, assessment wasn't made harder in the non-school setting, it was actually made simpler and was appropriate to the type of learning experiences going on. The most important thing I learnt about assessment during the placement is that the form it takes should be appropriate to the task being completed and that questioning, discussion, observation and outcome are all valid forms of assessment.

Consider:

- What strategies did Carolyn use to assess the children's and student's learning?
- Are there alternative strategies that she could also have used during the placement?

One of the purposes of assessment is to provide evidence of how children are progressing with their learning. It highlights where children have gaps in their knowledge and understanding and relevant action can be taken as a result. This is perfectly illustrated in the following case study extract.

Case Study: David – Traditional

Learning through play is an underlying principle of the Early Years Foundation Stage and this was most easily evidenced through summative assessment in the form of observations and photographs. I learnt that a key part of assessment in the Early Years was being able to recognise the skills that are being used and then placing these in the appropriate area of learning. Every term the number of profile points a child had gained in the appropriate area was then entered into a tracking system that collated all of the levels for every child across the school.

Case Study—Cont'd

It was through assessment that gaps in the curriculum were also identified. For example, if there were very few observations for Physical Development then this would be highlighted and fed back into the next planning meeting. Planning meetings also gave the teachers chance to raise any concerns they might have over the progress of certain children. The main concern was usually that certain children only accessed certain areas available. Ideas and activities were then usually brainstormed that would either engage with the child in a different aspect in their preferred area or entice them away to a different area. If these options failed then a play partner would focus on aiding and encouraging children to do different activities.

Consider:

- How can you keep written records to inform you of the children's progress?
- How would you try to ensure each child accessed all the areas?

Key points

- Talk to whoever will be able to give you advice and guidance on 'the basics' during the pre-placement preparation. This could be a teacher at the setting or a student or teacher who has been to the setting previously.
- Find out as much detail as possible about what you will be teaching.
- Focus on what children will learn, rather than what they will do.
- Gather sufficient and relevant resources to make your lessons interesting.
- Make sure you understand the behaviour management policy and other relevant policies, and know what strategies and requirements are expected, and strategies you will use.
- Include in your planning how you will assess the children and how this will inform future planning and practice.

Resources

www.behaviour4learning.ac.uk
www.qcda.gov.uk
www.standards.dfes.gov.uk
www.teachernet.gov.uk
www.ttrb.ac.uk

Overcoming the Challenges

Summary

We sincerely hope that all your placements are very positive and enjoyable ones. Occasionally thought there may be challenges to face and overcome. In the previous chapter we looked at getting the basics right, and in this chapter we move on to consider some aspects that may prove to be particularly challenging. Every placement setting is different and there are challenges that arise from the particular context. One school or setting may approach learning completely differently to another due to philosophy, style and resources. We will consider the challenge of differentiating work to enable all children to succeed.

Teaching is dynamic and unpredictable, as well as being based on relationships, which can be extremely variable. Thus, however well you plan and prepare you cannot possibly predict what is going to happen during a working day. The environment you are working in might not vary much but when you are working with people you can expect the unexpected. We will focus specifically on behaviour management and briefly on two issues we hope you do not have to face, child protection and bereavement. Finally, we will consider the challenges of language and communication particularly when working with children who have English as an additional language.

Differentiation

Teachers want all the children in their class to succeed. It therefore follows that in an ideal situation work should be differentiated so that all the children are challenged at an appropriate level. When you begin a placement, one of the first challenges is trying to find out the level at which the children are working. Your teacher may supply you with assessment results and you can have a look at the children's work in their books but, even with this information, it often takes a little while to be able to match the work appropriately. The following case study extract illustrates how difficult it is to differentiate work when working in large classes with few resources.

Case Study: Rachel – Gambia

The Gambian State, in response to the lack of resources, provided each school with a set of 3 text books per child; English, Mathematics and Social Studies. These books formed the basis of all teaching; the teachers educated the children using these books, taking learning objectives from them, until completed. They were similar to English schemes of work; however they offered no flexibility and no regular reviews. The head teacher informed me that teachers are 'encouraged to develop a scheme of work from which they can take their lesson plans'.

I did not see any differentiation of work in the Gambia. Classes were large and poorly resourced; the teacher had only one small chalkboard for the children to work from. To differentiate work would be have been very difficult; children would need to be split into groups and set different tasks, this would mean that only one group could work from the board while others would have to be taught verbally which may distract others from their work. The only way of providing children with the right level of work would be to individually set questions in their exercise books. This would be a significant change in teaching practice, and would be very time consuming for such large classes.

From my traditional placements I recognised that differentiation was vital when providing children with a quality education. However it was a lot easier to differentiate in English schools compared to the Gambia. Teachers create differentiated tasks for different groups or set individual targets to cater for the child's needs. The children are assessed against their own learning objective or against specific criteria. The resources and extra

Case Study—Cont'd

support provided in English classrooms make it easier to differentiate for the children. The Gambian classrooms we worked in had virtually no resources, very few teachers and there was certainly no extra help.

In the Gambia, the Department of State for Education (2006) suggested that teachers should teach using one of two methods, the presentation method or the enquiry method. The presentation method was regarded as the most efficient way of making sure all pupils can learn when they are part of a large class. Indeed other methods would be harder to use with very limited resources and very large classes. The enquiry method includes problem solving, experimenting, role play, carrying out surveys and pupils posing their own questions, the children are told less but are encouraged to find out for themselves, to learn by doing and therefore to learn and remember. However, the children had outdated books as their only resource, which meant that using the enquiry method would be very difficult to implement.

Consider:

- What were the issues that Rachel faced with regard to differentiation, during her placement?
- How might such issues be addressed?

Of course, a student on a placement is not expected to change the way a school operates and there were limited options for Rachel. However, when circumstances allow, it is possible to differentiate in a number of ways. You can differentiate by the questions that you pose as well as by the work that you set the children to do. The following case study extract illustrates how differentiation can be imaginatively introduced even when the spread of ability is wide.

Case Study: Carolyn – Traditional

I began the planning process by addressing the first of my many challenges – how to plan for a mixed age class. Initially I didn't know where to start, as I was so used to taking topics from the National Strategies for the appropriate year group I was teaching and planning around those. Now, I had two year groups to accommodate and didn't have a clue which topics I should teach. I wasn't sure whether I should be looking at Year 3 topics, Year 4 topics or both.

Case Study—Cont'd

Luckily for me, help was at hand. Teachers at the school informed me they worked on a two year cycle so that all of the topics recommended by the National Primary Strategy and QCA could be covered without any children having to do the same topic again during their second year in the same class. The idea was that during the year, you would teach half of the topics from year 3 and half of the topics from year 4. Then the following year, you would teach the other topics you had missed. And so on, the cycle would continue so that all of the children accessed all of the topics. The school was also registered with 'The Hamilton Trust' which provided examples of mixed age planning and access to resources. So there was plenty of help and resources available to me.

However, although the school had found a way to cover topics and curriculum areas for mixed-age classes, it hadn't provided for the fact that whatever topic you taught, you would have to teach it at multiple levels so that it was accessible yet challenging for all of the pupils in the class. For example, when teaching the Numeracy topic 'Rounding, Estimating and Measuring' I had to ensure I planned activities that were challenging enough for the more able year 4 children, appropriate for the less able year 4s and more able year 3s while still being accessible for the less able year 3s. All while covering the same objectives for everybody.

This was indeed, a challenge, but I did find a successful way of dealing with such extensive differentiation. The trick was to break each objective down into levels of success criteria for each lesson. In a lesson where the main objective was 'To round numbers to the nearest 10, 100 & 1000'. I used different levels of success criteria to assess the children against at the end of the lesson, such as:

– I can round 2 digit numbers to the nearest 10.
– I can round 2 and 3 digit numbers to the nearest 10 and 100.
– I can round 3 digit numbers to the nearest 100.
– I can round 3 and 4 digit numbers to the nearest 100 and 1000.

This allowed me to differentiate my teaching accordingly so that all of the children in the class could be challenged at an appropriate level within the same lesson. This was the most important thing I learnt about planning, that regardless of the topic or subject, the lessons must be differentiated so that all children are challenged appropriately while still maintaining a sense of inclusion by adapting the same learning objective to suit everybody.

Consider:

● What were the challenges Carolyn faced with regard to differentiation?
● How did she differentiate for a mixed age class?

Behaviour management

Behaviour management is one of the toughest challenges for all student teachers whether on a traditional placement, an alternative placement or an international placement. It is also very frustrating, because even when you have a good day and think that you have finally mastered this skill, the next day it can all go wrong again. If you are a sculptor and working with a piece of clay, however many times you start a new piece, the clay will be basically the same and all you need to do is improve your skills. However, as a teacher, you are working with children who can be very different one day than they were the previous day, so it is not just about you improving your skills. Understanding this is extremely important because when you evaluate a lesson where behaviour management has been an issue, it is no use simply concentrating on what you did or should have done. You need also to consider whether there were any other reasons for the challenging behaviour.

The following case study was based in a Special school. Although you may never undertake a placement in a Special school the reason for including this particular case study is because it illustrates very clearly how evaluating the reasons for challenging behaviour can give vital insight into how to manage it.

Case Study: Sally – Special school

Behaviour management was a challenge I identified very early on in the placement. Most of the behaviours encountered were physical including biting, hitting, grabbing and hair pulling, although some others such as spitting and refusal were witnessed.

In order to prepare for this the staff taught me a few key techniques such as standing side on to the child, making sure you do not back yourself or the pupil into a corner and the use of key command words such as 'Stop' instead of the word 'No' which antagonised some children further. I was very apprehensive that this was all I was 'armed' with when facing such behaviours. However, the setting believed that having to react to the behaviours like those discussed above, was not a situation that should arise often. They took a very proactive approach to behaviour management and encouraged me to do likewise. The staff introduced me to a new way of looking at behaviour – the notion that every behaviour had an antecedent and that if records were kept of the behaviours and events leading up to the incidents

Case Study—Cont'd

then 'flash points' within sessions could be easily identified. By recognizing this I could plan strategies into my sessions to eliminate or reduce the chances of the behaviour occurring.

Prior to this placement my behaviour management had always focused on reacting once an undesirable behaviour had been displayed. While this notion of being proactive about behaviour was liberating, it was also challenging because with the realisation that every behaviour had a purpose and that it was often a reaction to something in the environment, came the realisation that effectively I had the biggest role in preventing it. When behaviours did occur it was uncomfortable to consider the incident and look for the antecedent as it often meant it was something that I, or other staff, could have done to prevent it happening. However, the Unit staff were very constructive and the supportive and positive atmosphere made the process very efficient and effective.

The most important thing I learnt about behaviour management on this placement was that if I look for antecedents and considered strategies for removing or avoiding known antecedents then undesirable behaviour does decrease and I can spend less time reacting to behaviour and more time teaching.

Consider:

- What were the challenges faced by Sally during her placement?
- How did she address these challenges?

Some of the antecedents for inappropriate behaviour are not within your control. For example, some teachers may say that children's behaviour is worse on a windy day, and also on a wet day when children have not been able to go out and play. You cannot control the weather, but you can speak to your class teacher and make changes to planned activities to take into account that children are more lively than usual.

The reasons for inappropriate behaviour may relate to something that affects the whole class, such as wet playtimes, school concerts or approaching the end of term. It is equally likely that the reasons may be personal to an individual child. There are many factors outside of school that influence a child's behaviour. Consider the following questions:

- Has the child had enough sleep before coming to school?
- Has the child eaten breakfast?
- Is the child's family situation stable?
- Is there an illness in the family?

You may not know the answer to these questions, but it is often the case that factors outside of school are the reason for challenging behaviour in school. If you are aware of difficulties you can speak with the teacher and there may be actions that can be taken to give extra support to the child.

Child protection

Inappropriate behaviour at school can sometimes be a sign that there are potential issues outside school. This is a very sensitive area and one that, as a student, you would normally not be involved with. However, if you are teaching for a significant proportion of the day you may notice something that causes you concern .There are many signs that may indicate that a child is being abused but equally those signs may indicate something completely different so it is very important not to jump to conclusions.

The following is a list of some signs that might indicate abuse and is taken from the Kidscape website, www.kidscape.org.uk.

Physical abuse

- Unexplained recurrent injuries or burns
- Improbable excuses or refusal to explain injuries
- Wearing clothes to cover injuries, even in hot weather
- Refusal to undress for gym
- Aggression towards others
- Fear of physical contact – shrinking back if touched

Sexual abuse

- Being overly affectionate or knowledgeable in a sexual way inappropriate to the child's age
- Personality changes such as becoming insecure or clinging
- Being isolated or withdrawn
- Inability to concentrate
- Become worried about clothing being removed
- Suddenly drawing sexually explicit pictures
- Trying to be 'ultra-good' or perfect; overreacting to criticism

Emotional abuse

- Sudden speech disorders
- Overreaction to mistakes

- Extreme fear of any new situation
- Extremes of passivity or aggression

Neglect

- Constant hunger
- Poor personal hygiene
- Constant tiredness
- Poor state of clothing

On a short placement you are unlikely to notice some of these signs, but there are some that may become apparent to you. Most importantly, if you are at all suspicious or concerned you should speak to a teacher about your concerns. Every school has a child protection policy and a designated teacher for child protection issues. Do not try and investigate situations yourself. Your responsibility is to pass your concerns to the teacher.

It is very unlikely, but possible, that a child may disclose to you that he or she is being abused. If that should happen, you should listen carefully to what the child is saying. You should not ask any leading questions nor promise to keep the information secret. As soon as you can, you should write down what the child has told you, in the child's own words or as closely as you can recall this, and go immediately to the teacher and pass the information on, so that it can be investigated by designated staff in the school or setting.

Bereavement

We hope that you never have to deal with child protection issues, and certainly not bereavement. It is extremely rare for a student teacher to experience bereavement in a school or setting, but it does occasionally happen. It may be that a teacher dies or a pupil or a family member of a pupil. The school is a community and when someone dies within that community it affects everyone. If you are on a placement at such a time you will be part of that community.

The head teacher, teachers and adults will take responsibility for actions that need to take place such as informing everyone, having special assemblies and often getting specialist support into the school, such as counsellors. You need to be particularly sensitive at such a time because not only will the pupils be distressed but the teachers may also be very upset. Recently, a student was on placement when a child in her class was killed in a road accident. She still had several weeks to complete the placement, and the school was happy for her to do so.

One of the most important skills and aspects for her to develop was the need to be flexible. She had lessons planned that she could not teach because lots of things changed and sometimes at short notice. She was very professional and worked with her class teacher supporting the pupils and doing what she was asked to do. Her placement provider gave immediate support so she knew she had someone to speak to, if needed. As a result, she successfully completed her placement, under very difficult circumstances, and learned things she didn't expect to when the placement began.

We will not consider the practicalities of what to do in a school or setting when there is a bereavement. However, if you wish to find out more information, the following websites give help and support to schools in dealing with bereavement issues:

www.childbereavement.org.uk
www.crusebereavementcare.org.uk
www.rd4u.org.uk [for young people]
www.winstonswish.org.uk

Working with other adults

It is likely that you will find working with other adults quite a challenge, particularly if the other adults are much more experienced than you are. There are many adults who make up the staff of a school and you need to form good relationships with them, as far as that is possible.

Teaching assistants (TAs), learning support assistants (LSAs), specialist teaching assistants (STAs) and higher level teaching assistants (HLTAs) and learning mentors (LMs) are just a few of the adults now working with individual pupils or as general support in classrooms. It is very important to recognize that they are trained professionals and may have many years of experience. Make sure you talk with your teacher about the roles of the other adults in the classroom and clarify what is expected of you. Normally, you will be expected to plan for the other adults and to make sure that they understand in advance of the lesson what you expect them to do. By giving the other adults a copy of your lesson plan with information on it of what you expect from them, you will demonstrate that you value them and regard their role as a vital part of the lesson.

In the following case study extract you will see how other adults can take on a number of roles and be extremely helpful to you as the teacher.

Case Study: Sally – Special school

I began the placement by working with individuals and/or small groups of children. Towards the end of the first week I undertook team teaching with the class teacher. I particularly enjoyed taking part in, and contributing to, teaching teams in this way. It gave me the opportunity and the confidence to try new things, in a supportive environment and to learn from and draw on the experiences and expertise of those around me. It enabled me to understand more fully the importance of good communication between staff and the significant role that additional adults have in the classroom environment.

All of this helped me when I eventually progressed to teaching groups and ultimately the whole class independently and was having to plan for the deployment of additional adults. Many things were enhanced by the support of additional adults. For instance, when undertaking assessment many of them were able to take pictures or jot down notes about some-thing a child had said or done which I might have missed– they were like a second pair of eyes and ears. However, in order to obtain optimum benefit from them it was important to have procedures in place for them to share their information with me.

The Unit had a scheme whereby each child had an A4 piece of paper on the wall and any notes made by the teacher or additional adults could be stuck up there. These were collected at the end of the session or day by the teacher and used to inform planning and then added to the child's assessment file for evidence in summative assessments. Additional adults also played a significant role in behaviour management. They were often able to spot antecedents and could offer different perspectives on any behavioural incidents.

Consider:

- How can you try to develop effective working relationships with colleagues and adults in your placement setting?
- If there are potential issues with regard to a particular relationship, what strategies could you use to try to improve the situation?

Language and communication

One of the most immediate challenges faced by teachers is whether the children or students will understand them, and whether they will be able to communicate with them. In many schools and settings there are children and students who speak English as an additional language (EAL). Some may be able to speak English fluently, while others may have very limited English or none at all. This may also be true of their parents/guardians, family and members of the local community. If you undertake an international placement to a non-English speaking country, you should expect that many or at least some of the children and adults will speak very limited or no English. This needs to be a consideration before each placement you undertake, even if you speak a number of different languages, as demonstrated in the following case study.

Case Study: Jaz – India

The international experience has positively impacted on my professional development. Within S Public School, collaboration has proved to be an essential approach to teaching. By working together, we were able to develop, maintain, and progress not only learning, but also relationships with children. This allowed us to establish high expectations, which challenged us to consider the children's abilities and skills. In developing a mural project, in particular, I learned about how constructive the English National Curriculum can be when considering how to monitor, plan for, and evaluate children's learning.

This international experience contributed to my critical reflection of my pedagogy with regard to identifying potential barriers that can result when working with EAL children, but also highlighted alternative ways to communicate in order to understand the potential that the children possessed. Specific consideration was given to 'Q18 – Understand[ing] how children and young people develop and that the progress and well-being of learners are affected by a range of developmental, social, religious, ethnic, cultural, and linguistic influences' (TDA, 2008, p.10).

Before this placement, I did not anticipate having difficulties in communicating with the children as I fluently speak English, Punjabi, and Hindi. However, I did not account for the variety of dialects and the impact these would have on misunderstanding. This made me reflect on the way that I communicate not only with children, but with all individuals and emphasised the need to use a consistent clear voice, supporting gestures, and visual aids. This experience has made me appreciate the international setting and the reasons for the differences in procedures that are followed. Fundamentally, this experience will improve my own pedagogy because it has strengthened my understanding of England's National Curriculum and how I can teach diverse learners more effectively.

Consider:

- Why was Jaz surprised that there were language issues during his placement?
- How can you develop and improve your language and communication skills prior to placement?

Naomi had undertaken two short visits to the Gambia, which led her to choosing to return there for her international placement. She had initial concerns about language and communication, but with support and guidance was able to overcome potential barriers. She gained such an incredible experience that she has decided that she would like to work in the Gambia once she has gained QTS.

Case Study: Naomi – Gambia

I spent ten weeks working in schools in the Gambia, and with a child protection officer. I knew from my first two visits that I wanted to complete a longer placement there to gain a better understanding of the culture and education. The children within the settings all spoke their tribal language first, and English second, sometimes third, so communication could be challenging at times. However I learnt many strategies to make the situation easier. I developed my ability to think and teach creatively, due to a lack of resources and communication issues, which meant I needed to be able to adapt lessons and activities on the spot, and change focus and teaching strategy, to enable learning. My placement was a life changing experience, and had a huge impact on me personally and professionally. I am a much more confident person and feel able to challenge pre conceptions and expectations, based on real life examples and situations. But more than that I think that we had an impact on the children's lives, and I hope to be able to continue to do this in the future.

Consider:

- What did Naomi learn during the placement that impacted on her personal and professional development?
- How can you develop 'creative' communication skills prior to placement?

English as an Additional Language (EAL) & Modern Foreign Languages (MFL)

During the placement it is useful to keep a 'learning journal' as outlined in Chapter 4, and if a requirement of the placement, you can use the journal to track your progress against QTS Standards or equivalent legislation. One particular QTS Standard that many students find difficult to evidence relates to working with children with English as an Additional Language (EAL), with whom the students have had limited or no previous experience.

(TDA, 2008) Q19:

> Know how to make effective personalized provision for those they teach, including those for who English is an additional language or who have special educational needs or disabilities and how to take practical account of diversity and promote equality and inclusion in their teaching

One student who undertook a placement in a German speaking school in Austria noted:

> As the Grade 1 class had very limited experience in English it was important that teaching involved lots of kinetics or communication by bodily movement. These actions enabled us to praise the children and to show them that what they were doing was right. We demonstrated a game using your hands, which the children followed without having to communicate verbally. Modelling what we wanted the children to do enabled them to do tasks, and non-verbal communication was used to show praise.
>
> The placement enabled me to appreciate the difficulties children with English as an additional language (EAL) in English schools may face. I found that from observing lessons taught in German that a small basic picture can help explain an idea significantly and body language and 'acting' out can really help understanding. I now know what the saying 'A picture paints a thousand words' really means.

The DFES (2005) stated that:

> The cornerstone of the National Languages Strategy is the introduction of language learning in all primary schools by 2010. This means that all pupils throughout KS2 will have the opportunity to learn a foreign language and develop their interest in the culture of other nations.

Thus, from 2010 all pupils in KS2 needed to be taught a foreign language, and indeed many primary schools had already been teaching a foreign language for a number of years. This can be a very daunting proposition for many students training to be teachers, even for those with some knowledge and skills in another language. Some of the students who decided to participate in an international placement cited one of the reasons for doing this was to develop their language skills and their professional ability to be able to teach a foreign language in school, and to gain confidence in being able to do so.

One student, having completed a placement in an Austrian School, stated:

> The placement also allowed me to see how modern foreign languages (MFL) can be taught in primary schools, as this was an area I had no previous experience of. I now feel more confident to teach MFL, and recognise the importance of developing conversational skills and being able to give children practical knowledge of a language that they can use. The children were really excited about using the English they had learned and wanted to ask and answer questions in English. 'Learners attitudes to learning and their confidence in themselves as learners are key factors in successful learning. Feeling confident to have a go, without fear of failure, and developing a positive attitude to learning itself allows learners to develop confidence in their ability to learn', (Gibbons, 2002, p11). This is a key idea, particularly when teaching languages. The children were encouraged to speak and answer as best they could and to develop confidence in 'having a go'.

A colleague who also went to a school in Austria noted:

> With MFL becoming statutory in KS2, the experience really developed my language skills and my confidence in speaking other languages. It has also given me a great deal of understanding about children who do not speak English – we had to undertake a lot of translation and it really emphasised the issues that children with EAL must face in school. The insights I have gained will aid my teaching pupils with EAL and pupils with SEN who may struggle to understand concepts. Teaching RE in English and German (with pupils between 6–11 in two schools) also gave me more confidence in my specialist subject area.

David concluded that his placement in Japan was:

> a fantastic experience and gave me a lot of food for thought both within an education and social context. There was a language barrier (I had taken Japanese lessons from a Japanese student for a few months before travelling) but all the children and staff were very welcoming. I taught English and joined in with extra-curricular activities. I saw a range of different approaches, which will impact on my own teaching, and very different relationships between staff. The 1500 word assignment has not justified my experience, and don't hold me to it, but I could have easily written 5000!

Key points

- Meeting individual needs within a school or setting can be a challenge, so consider ways of differentiating activities, tasks, resources, instructions, support and guidance to best address these.

- Understanding the reasons for inappropriate behaviour will help you to manage it within the classroom or setting. Ask for advice if necessary, and take the opportunity to observe and learn from other teachers.
- Ensure that you have an underpinning knowledge of child protection and associated issues, and that you know who to speak to if you have any concerns. Note and date accurately if a child or student discloses any issues to you.
- Working with other adults can be very rewarding and beneficial to the pupils and to you, but relationships need time, effort and the ability to listen, to work well.
- Effective communication, verbal and non-verbal, is vital for any placement – so be prepared to explore ways of communicating when and if there are barriers such as language or disability.

Resources

www.behaviour4learning.ac.uk
www.tda.gov.uk
www.teachernet.gov.uk

National Society of Prevention of Cruelty to Children (NSPCC): 0800 800 5000

8

When Things Do Not Go to Plan

Summary

Nothing in life always goes to plan and that includes placements. You may prepare thoroughly and work very hard, but that does not guarantee a placement will go well as there may be factors that are outside your control. Usually the aspects that do not go to plan are minor and are easily resolved, but sometimes they can be more serious.

This chapter looks in detail at the variety of challenges that can arise on placements. We will demonstrate how important it is to identify exactly what the causes of a problem are. Once this is known then it is possible to consider solutions, and we will look at various scenarios and key actions that could be undertaken. It is extremely important to prioritize actions to ensure that progress is made quickly. We will also consider what sources of help are available to you before and during your placement. This will include help from your school or setting, from your training provider and also from outside sources. If you are unsuccessful on a placement we will consider what options are open to you. We will offer advice concerning resitting placements and also on what other options are available to you.

Most students begin a placement with great confidence and expect to be successful. However, there can be difficulties, and these can arise in many different situations. The most important point is to recognize when there is a problem, because denial tends to make situations much more difficult. Only when you acknowledge a problem can you begin to work on addressing the issues.

Analysing the situation

When you realize that a placement is not going as well as you would hope, you need to carefully examine what is happening. Sometimes you can do this on your own, but it can also be very useful to involve others and discuss issues with a peer or colleague. The first question you need to address is, 'what exactly is going wrong?' Although this may seem a simple question to answer, it is not always simple at all. There may be many issues that are having an impact on you. Thus, it may be helpful to consider the following questions:

- Have you had similar difficulties on previous placements?
- Do the difficulties relate to your relationship with the teacher or mentor?
- Do the difficulties relate to your relationships with the children?
- Is the behaviour of the children an issue?
- Are the children enjoying your lessons?
- Do you understand what is expected of you?

Once you have identified what you consider the issues to be, you need to analyse how you arrived at this situation, before you can start addressing the issues. You must recognize that your understanding of the situation may be inaccurate, and be prepared to change your original stance.

It is important to be reflective and honest with yourself. It does not help to blame others, especially if you recognize that you have probably not done what you could have done. It is worth considering the following questions:

- Were you fully prepared for the start of the placement?
- Have you been effective with your allocation of time and demonstrated effective time management?
- Have you demonstrated enthusiasm and willingness to act upon advice?
- Have you used your initiative to solve difficulties or have you expected others to tell you what to do?

These questions are all about you, because self reflection is always the best place to begin. Once you have considered these questions honestly you may well have a better insight as to the cause of the difficulties you face. However, you may be able to answer these questions positively so there may be other potential causes. It may be that the school or setting is expecting too much from you. Different placements have different demands and sometimes a school or setting may be unaware of exactly what is expected. Sometimes there may be a personality clash between you and the teacher or mentor. If you have considered all of these possibilities and still have not identified why things are not going well, it may be that your level of performance is not as effective as it needs to be.

Identify the key problems

It is very likely that if you have carefully considered all of the suggested questions raised, you will have decided that there is not one single cause of your difficulties, but several. It would be very surprising if there was only one reason. It is also very likely that there are several difficulties; so before you can really make progress with addressing them, you need to identify what the key problems are. Often, if you can address and resolve the key problems, everything else will fall into place. You need to take your time on this process, because very often the most obvious problems are not the key problems.

Consider the following examples:

Example 1

If you are struggling with behaviour management this will be very obvious, and you may think that you need to learn some new strategies. In practice, the key problem may be that your planning is not sufficient or the content of your lessons is too easy or too difficult. If that is the case, it will not make any difference just changing your behaviour management strategies. If you address the key problem and get your planning right, the behaviour of the children will improve because they will be motivated by the lessons.

Example 2

You may be struggling with record-keeping. You may be spending the majority of your time planning for the next lessons and preparing resources. The obvious problem is that you are not quick enough with your planning, whereas the key problem may be that you are working too many hours on your part-time job, to meet all the demands of your placement. By trying to reduce the hours you are working on your part-time job you will find time to do your record-keeping.

Example 3

You may be on an international placement or any distant placement that requires you to live away from home. Concentration on your work could be a challenge. You know you need to keep a better focus and get on with your work, but the key problem may simply be home sickness. Perhaps a phone call to your family at home would help you to feel better, and then concentrating on your work might be easier.

Example 4

Your placement is not going particularly well. You seem to struggle with planning, and then in the lessons the behaviour of the children is not appropriate. You know you need to improve the quality of your lessons including planning, resources and behaviour management. The key problem, however, may be that you don't really want to be a teacher. If that is the problem, it is very unlikely that you will be able to improve your teaching, because your heart is not in what you are doing. The best thing is to tell your mentor or teacher how you are feeling.

Example 5

Early in your placement, your mentor may have criticized some aspects of your teaching, such as subject knowledge. The weeks go by, and you become anxious that you are not good enough and you will never improve. In reality, your mentor may now be pleased with you, but the key problem is lack of communication. You assume she/he is still not pleased with you, and she/he assumes you know everything is alright because it has not been mentioned again. If you want to know whether you are improving, do not be afraid to ask.

These examples illustrate how often, when problems occur on placement, there are underlying issues that need to be resolved before anything else can change.

Prioritizing actions

Once you have fully analysed your situation and identified the key problems, you have to begin to rectify these, and this may seem very daunting. Most importantly, you must try to keep calm and address the issues in a systematic way. Knowing there is a problem and where to begin is often a challenge, and you will probably need help from your mentor to do this. If you find it difficult to talk with your mentor do not give up and think the situation is impossible. Talk to your class teacher, if he/she is not your mentor, or speak to a training provider tutor.

The following scenarios are based on issues or concerns that have arisen with students and demonstrate a variety of solutions to these. At the end of each scenario some key actions are highlighted. If you are struggling with the same challenges, these will point you towards actions you can take to improve the situation.

Key problem – planning

Student A was struggling with lesson planning. She had lots of ideas for activities but somehow her lessons were disjointed and often the children were not very motivated. After discussion it became apparent that student A had never fully understood the process of beginning a lesson plan with a clear learning outcome. She focused on what the children would do rather than on what they would learn. Once she started to focus on what the children would learn her activities suddenly had much more purpose. Her planning was also done much quicker, because she understood what she was trying to achieve.

Action plan
- Begin your lesson plan with a clear learning outcome.
- Plan activities that will help the children achieve the learning outcome.

Key problem – planning

Student B was very dispirited because the children in his class were not listening to him or respecting him as they should. Despite trying to use the behaviour management strategies that his teacher used and also others he had learned about, the behaviour of the children did not improve. When the situation was carefully analysed it became apparent that student B was not planning thoroughly. His lesson plans were brief and resources were poor. He spent time with his mentor and class teacher, learning what was expected. He began to plan lessons that were appropriately matched to the level of the children. His resources were greatly improved and once he started to address these key problems the behaviour of the children began to improve because they started to enjoy the lessons.

Action plan
- Use a lesson plan template provided by your training provider.
- Complete every section of the template so that your plan shows exactly what you hope will happen in the lesson.
- Prepare suitable resources that will interest and motivate the children.

Key problem – relationships with children

Student C was having significant problems with the behaviour of the children in her class. She tried to use appropriate strategies to manage behaviour, but these were not working. When the problem was analysed carefully it became obvious that when she was not teaching, student C spoke to the children more like a friend than a teacher. She did not correct inappropriate behaviour. Student C explained that one of her most important aims was for the children to like her. Consequently, she was being far too friendly, and not acting like a teacher at all times. Her mentor explained that if she was a good teacher the children would like her automatically. It was not easy, but student C stopped trying to be friendly and concentrated on being a good teacher and she began to earn the respect of the children.

Action plan
- Correct inappropriate behaviour.
- Keep a professional distance from the children and do not allow them to ask personal questions.
- Be firm and consistent, so that children know what you expect.
- Remember to use positive reinforcement.

Key problem – relationships with staff

Student D was finding her placement difficult in a number of ways. She reported to her training provider that she was not enjoying her placement at all, and was considering giving up. When the training provider tutor spoke with student D it became clear that she felt her teacher did not like her and did not want her in her classroom. Consequently, student D had lost motivation, she was not working as hard as she had at first and was starting to receive negative feedback from her mentor.

Importantly, she had alerted her tutor, who was able to intervene and listen to both sides of the story. In reality, the student had been overconfident and appeared arrogant on her first visit, and this had upset her teacher. The tutor was able to mediate and from then onwards, the situation greatly improved. Student D apologized for any arrogance she may have displayed and her teacher became much more supportive.

Action plan
- Alert your training provider tutor as soon as you think there is a serious problem.
- Be professional. If some of your actions or attitudes have caused a problem you should apologize.

- Do everything you can to be helpful and act upon the advice you are given.
- Show respect to your teacher and it is likely that this will be reciprocated.

Key problem – subject knowledge

Student E was criticized by her mentor because her subject knowledge was poor in more than one area, and she had taught misconceptions to the children. She knew this was an issue, but she did not know how to put it right. The problem seemed overwhelming. However, she identified the topics she needed to teach, and she went to the library to find books to help. The most helpful books were at GCSE level. They were not too difficult for her to understand and they gave her sufficient knowledge for her to feel confident when she was teaching.

Action plan
- Identify the topics you are expected to teach as soon as possible.
- Research the topics thoroughly, so that you understand what you are teaching.
- Use books and resources available from the school or from your training provider.

Key problem – behaviour management

Student F had difficulties from the start of his placement in managing the behaviour of the children. He spoke with his mentor and class teacher about the problem, and several issues were identified. When he gave explanations and instructions to the class he often was unaware that a good number of the children were still talking. He did not change his tone of voice; when he told the children to be quiet, so many of them ignored him. He also made threats about what would happen if the children continued to misbehave, but did not carry through his threats. After some discussion with his mentor, it was agreed that he needed to focus on three targets. When he wanted the attention of the class he needed to change the tone and volume of his voice so that he sounded as though he expected the children to listen. Secondly, he practised waiting for silence before he gave instructions, and thirdly, when he made a threat he followed it up. This remained a struggle for him throughout the placement, but significant progress was made and he passed.

Action plan
- Be fully aware of the school's discipline policy and how this should work in practice.
- Ensure all the children know your expectations for behaviour.

- Stop the lesson before you give instructions and wait for silence.
- Vary the tone and expression of your voice when you want the attention of the whole class.
- Think carefully before you make a threat, as you should be prepared to carry it through if necessary.
- Use praise when children respond appropriately to you.

Key problem – assessment

Student G was having a few problems planning and teaching interesting lessons. The children enjoyed her lessons and everything seemed to be going well. However, when questioned about how she assessed the children's learning, she admitted that she just looked at the books at the end of a lesson. Her mentor advised her that assessment by product was only one way of assessment. Targets were set for her to do some assessment by observation and some by discussion. This had to be planned and managed carefully, but she was able to make significant progress in this area.

Action plan

- In your lesson plan include which aspects of the children's learning you are going to specifically assess (based on the learning outcomes), how you are going to do this, where and how the assessments will be recorded and how you will use this to inform your future planning and practice.
- Plan to use appropriate and different assessment methods, such as observation and discussion when working with a small group.
- Ask your class teacher for help in how to plan and manage assessment using different methods, and how these can be used to aid further learning.

Key problem – record-keeping

Student H was progressing well on placement until asked to show his mentor his record keeping. It was non-existent, and this was largely due to the fact that he did not know what was expected of him. As the school did not have one set way of record-keeping he was given the opportunity to meet with several teachers and see how they kept their records. It was also pointed out to him that there was guidance from his training provider on how to keep records in his placement booklet. The second issue was that he did not understand why he had to keep records. He regarded record-keeping as a chore that the training provider tutors expected him to do and he saw no connection between record-keeping and teaching. When he realized that his record-keeping was actually a tool to help him with his planning and was evidence of whether the children were learning, he gave it a higher priority, and with the guidance of his mentor he was able to produce useful records.

Action plan

- When you begin the planning process ensure that you consider how you are going to keep records.
- Prepare suitable templates before the placement begins.
- Keep your records simple and easy to understand. Always include your learning outcomes.
- Record-keeping should be a regular part of your planning, teaching, evaluation and assessment cycle and have a positive impact on learning.
- Consider how your assessments will inform future planning and practice.

Student I: Key problem – time management

Student I was full of enthusiasm and ideas. She had so many ideas that she found it extremely difficult to plan lessons and teach them in the available time. Frequently, her introductions were too long, as she did not want to miss anything out. As a result, the children usually did not have enough time to do their work. A plenary was often missed out because the children had not completed their work or student I simply had not noticed the time. After talking with her mentor, she identified that she was trying to fit too many learning outcomes into her lessons. She was also underestimating how long it takes children to do various tasks. When she cut back on the content, the children were able to complete the work and she was able to have a plenary at the end of each lesson to reinforce the learning.

Action plan

- Limit your learning outcomes to one or two most significant ones.
- Your introduction should not be long. Observe your class teacher and make sure your introductions are no longer than his/hers.
- Allow sufficient time for the children to complete the tasks you set. Have an extension task ready for those who finish earlier that you would have predicted.
- Allow time at the end of a lesson to have a plenary session so that you can reinforce the learning outcome/s.

In each of these scenarios it was very important to draw up an action plan. Difficult problems can become manageable once an action plan is decided upon. As well as discussing a plan, it is also important to give your best efforts.

It is also necessary to look after yourself. When things are not going well and you start to worry, you are tempted to go without food because you have too much to do. You then stay up too late trying to do all your work and very quickly you make yourself ill. You need to eat and sleep!! Part of a good action plan should be a timetable that you stick to, that should include mealtimes, and a cut-off time when you stop work and try to relax.

Sources of help

We have already indicated how important it is to have assistance when things are not going to plan, and in this section we will look more closely at the many sources of help that are available to you. In a traditional school placement, you may have a mentor and part of his/her role is to give you help and support. Do not be afraid to tell your mentor, if there are things you do not understand. It is not at all uncommon for students to agree with all the advice given by a mentor when they don't really understand what is being asked of them. In the long run, this is not helpful and leads to greater problems. Sometimes you may find it difficult to talk to your mentor. In this case, you should try to speak with your teacher, if this is a different person, or there may be another teacher in the school you find you can talk to, especially in larger schools where there may be a parallel class or other teachers teaching the same subject in secondary school.

If you are undertaking an alternative or international placement you may not have an official mentor, but there should be a named person in the school/ setting who has responsibility for you. Although there are others who can help you, it is much easier if the help is available in your school or setting, because the staff are there all the time. There may be situations where you feel able to speak to the head teacher or manager of the setting to ask for help. This will depend upon the circumstances, but they want you to succeed and will want to give you support when they can. However, you should also contact your training provider if there are any potential issues, so that they are able to support you in dealing with these.

You will have a training provider tutor as a link when on a traditional placement, and a tutor may visit you while on an alternative or international placement. These tutors are often invaluable when there are issues or problems. However, you need to let them know there are potential problems, as soon as possible. Sometimes a telephone call or e-mail from a tutor can quickly sort out a misunderstanding and save a lot of heartache. If you wait until your tutor visits or contacts you, to raise problems, it may be that you do not have as much time to talk as you would like. To avoid this, you should be proactive. Find out your tutor's name and contact details before the placement. You can then explain the situation by e-mail or telephone, before they visit and before the situation escalates.

For some international and alternative placements you may not have a tutor coming to visit you. Nevertheless, you should have access to e-mail so you can seek help from your tutors. If you have a 'buddy' who undertook a similar placement the year before, they would be ideal to contact. Sometimes what you need is the opportunity to talk about the challenges you are facing. You will often feel more positive once you have shared your feelings and other students will not only listen but may be able to give you valuable advice that helps you move forward.

The nature of the challenges you are facing obviously determines the kind of help that you need. If you are lacking in ideas for your lessons you should make time to discover what resources are available at your school or setting. In traditional placements there will probably be a whole range of resources including books, CDs, DVDs, interactive whiteboards and many other practical resources. Most training provider libraries have resources that you can borrow so you should not be short of resources. If you are on an international placement this may not be the case, so planning in advance is vital, as discussed in Chapter 3.

The internet is also a vast source for resource material. However, you can waste a huge amount of time on it by searching randomly for information. At the end of this chapter, we have listed a number of useful websites that you can access. It is certainly not an exhaustive list, and you may find other useful sites. It is very important at this point to ensure that you are cautious when using plans you find on the internet. At first, this may seem like the answer to a lot of your challenges, but it is very difficult to teach from someone else's plans unless you have spent sufficient time to fully understand them. Certainly use the ideas and suggestions but do ensure that you understand the plans you are using in order to have autonomy over your planned activities. Writing them out in your own format is a good way to help you understand them.

A useful source of help is Teachers TV. The website address is: www.teachers. tv/. In addition to the website, Teachers TV programmes are available on the TV Channel on Sky 880, Virgin Media 240, Freesat 650 and, most recently, through iTunes U. Teachers TV supports the professional development of anyone working in school through videos, practical resources and an active online community. The programmes available cover a vast range of topics and for most of the challenges you may be facing there will be a programme or several programmes you can watch to support you. Most of the programmes are fairly short and can give you very practical help.

Possible next steps

Despite your best efforts, sometimes placements are unsuccessful and this can be a very distressing experience. If you are in this situation, you need time to reflect and recover before you make any major decisions about what to do next. You also need to calmly discuss the placement with your tutor. Do not rush into these discussions as you will probably be feeling emotional and not very level headed. When you feel that you have recovered sufficiently to think about your future in a calm and balanced way, there are some important questions that you need to reflect upon:

- What were the main reasons for failing the placement?
- If you had a fresh start, could you do better next time?
- Were the issues particular to that school or setting?
- Would a different school or setting make a difference?
- Do you still want to be a teacher?

As you consider these questions carefully, you need to be honest with yourself. Teaching is not an easy career and, unless you really want to be a teacher, it may not be sensible to continue. However, there are students who, despite difficulties, are still determined to pursue their dream of being a teacher.

If you want to try again, you will probably be offered a resit opportunity in a different school or setting. This is usually dependent on the outcome of an Examination Board held by your training provider. Students who have failed a placement are now successful teachers, so be positive and learn from an unsuccessful placement. The learning that takes place due to an unsuccessful placement can be immense. Meet with your tutor and make an action plan to ensure that you prepare yourself as best you possibly can for your resit. You may want to go into a school on a voluntary basis to build your confidence back up, before starting a resit placement.

It may be that after reflecting on the questions given here, you decide that teaching is not for you. Realizing this can be a great relief for students who know that this is the right decision. It is also very important to recognize that there is no such thing as a wasted experience. You will have learned a lot at whatever stage of your course you are on, and you need to keep this in mind as you consider the future.

There are many possibilities open to you and it is advisable to talk with a careers adviser before making a decision. If you are an undergraduate student, there may be a degree course that you can transfer to without moving from your training provider. Think carefully about the type of degree course you want to transfer to. Whether you are an undergraduate or postgraduate student, there are many jobs that involve working with children without having the responsibility of a teacher. Becoming a Teaching Assistant is an option, but being a nursery nurse, working in an after-school club or a sports centre or becoming a social worker could be other possible options. Whatever you decide to do in the future, always remember, although you did not complete the placement successfully, it does not mean that you are unsuccessful as a person or a professional. You have simply discovered that teaching may not be the career for you. You have skills and abilities that will enable you to do a different job or follow an alternative career successfully. So take the positive things with you and enjoy your future.

Key points

- Analyse the situation. What exactly is going wrong?
- Ask for help and support as soon as you recognize there are issues.
- Identify the key problem. Often one key problem leads to other problems.
- Make an action plan and prioritize your actions.
- If you are unsuccessful on a placement try not to make hasty decisions. Get advice and thoroughly consider your options.
- If you decide that teaching is not for you, your experiences will not be wasted. Take what you have learned and let it help you in whatever you do in the future.

Resources

http://nationalstrategies.standards.dcsf.gov.uk/primary/primaryframework/
http://publications.education.gov.uk
http://tre.ngfl.gov.uk
www.bbc.co.uk/schools/
www.behaviour4learning.ac.uk
www.channel4learning.com/index.html
www.mape.org.uk/activities/index.htm
www.qcda.gov.uk
www.ttrb.ac.uk

Part III
Reflecting on Your Experience

9

A Life-changing Experience?

Summary

Irrespective of the outcome of your placement, the experience you have gained will have an impact on your personal, professional and academic development. By the end of the placement you will know, understand and be able to do more than you could before you started. Thus, even if the experience is different from your expectations, or there were negative aspects or issues, you will have gained a significant amount. When you complete the placement you need to take time to reflect on the experience as a whole, and specific elements of it. There will have been successful and unsuccessful aspects of your placement; placements reflect real life. But how you deal with these, and the ability to reflect and analyse, will determine the impact that the experience has on you as an individual and you as a professional.

Each placement will be unique, and you will gain significantly different experiences. However all of these will be valuable, and have the potential to be life enhancing and even life changing. Fully immersing yourself in the placement and taking every opportunity to gain 'experiences' will be an excellent starting point. But 'living' the placement, and making the most of every situation, will make the difference between a successful placement and an incredible one.

Just as each placement will be distinct, so the impact that the placement has on your development will be individual to you. You can enjoy a placement; you can take the opportunity to explore new places and situations; you can develop new teaching strategies and approaches to learning and teaching; but how will you ensure that these have a positive impact on your development?

The importance of taking time to really reflect, review, consider, discuss, share, analyse and evaluate various aspects of your placement cannot be stressed enough. It will be through doing this, that you will be able to think about the impact that the experience can and will have on your development.

In this chapter we explore a few of the factors from placements that could have a significant impact on your personal and professional development. These include the impact of the learning environment; creative learning opportunities; working as part of a team on professional development; the impact of placements on personal development; the impact of 'being a learner'; and the role of subject knowledge and expertise on academic development.

Impact of the learning environment on professional development

As teacher trainers we often discuss the importance of effective learning environments. The environment in which children and students develop and learn is paramount to ensuring that their needs can be met and achieved. Appropriate buildings, rooms, indoor and outdoor space, resources, facilities, training and provision are significant elements of a school or setting. It is also vital to ensure a safe and secure environment which provides opportunities for exploration and challenge, and encourages the building of confidence and self-esteem.

Johanna, undertook an alternative placement in a study centre, which specialized in Outdoor Learning and Forest Schools. The environment was specifically designed to encourage creative activities, but provided Johanna with inspiration for her traditional placements.

Case Study: Johanna – Study Centre

My main focus was Forest Schools as I am interested in creative teaching and learning. When observing Forest School practitioners the focus was child led free play. Children developed socially and emotionally, physically, increased self awareness, independence, developed a positive attitude and increased self esteem and confidence.

I was amazed how much learning had taken place when children were offered a positive outdoor learning experience. The children learnt so much from the sessions and I was surprised how the activities naturally made links to elements of the National Curriculum. The groups' sizes were between 8 and 12, and I was able to build amazing relationships with the children, as the activities were based on developing new skills and risk management.

Case Study—Cont'd

I assisted and participated in many activities including, rock climbing, high ropes and rope swinging, archery, survival skills, build a camp fire, shelter building, mini-beat hunting, nature numeracy, nature music and environmental art. The placement was great and I have gained a real insight on how to deliver both Outdoor Learning and Forest School. Since the placement,I have worked with many Forest School practitioners and have delivered many outdoor learning activities in several schools. I have created a Forest School area in two schools and am hoping to achieve a Forest Schools level 3 practitioners award, which will lead me to Forest Schools Level 4 Training. This will enable me to train other teachers and people who are interested in delivering a Forest School programme.

Consider:

- Can you identify skills and understanding that Johanna developed as a result of her placement?
- How could a Forest School approach be adapted for a traditional setting?

While we believe that these aspects of the learning environment are significant, we also need to consider situations where such an environment is fundamentally different. For example, a placement in a developing country may be initially shocking and disturbing, but can also be enlightening and change our ideas and perceptions.

Case Study: Rachel – Gambia

The Department of State for Education in the Gambia (2006) is striving to improve education and note that teachers know that quality education is the key to the development in the Gambia. My time in Gambia was a wonderful learning experience and a beneficial adventure. It confirmed my belief in the importance of a safe, secure and positive learning environment and the impact that this has on the child's attitude and ability to learn. It also consolidated my previous learning and added to my professional development by demonstrating to me how important it is to have adequate resources, carefully differentiated in order to engage and stimulate the children, so that they are fully involved in their learning. It has shown me the value of a positive, comfortable and efficient classroom environment; an area where children are happy and eager to learn.

Case Study—Cont'd

The English schools I have experience of are very well resourced in comparison to the schools we visited in the Gambia. We need to use these resources effectively to give all the children the best opportunities to learn. Differentiation is essential for the success of each child. We should set work according to the needs of the class; target individuals who are underachieving, encourage and motivate the class to make sure they achieve to the best of their ability.

My placement in the Gambia made me realise that the English educational system is effective and well resourced; and that we have many facilities to offer our children. It made me want to strive to be a better teacher and to provide for our children in a way that cannot be so readily provided in other countries.

When you review your placement, consider the following questions:

- Which elements do you consider significant in the development of an effective learning environment?
- Were these elements present in your placement?
- If some of these elements were not present how you did overcome this, to try to create a good learning environment?
- How could you use this experience to impact on your professional development?

Impact of 'creativity' on professional development

It always seems easy to say make your lessons and activities more creative and fun, but as with planning any lessons or activities, thought, time and effort needs to be given to this. The more reading and research you can undertake concerned with creativity the better; the more opportunities you have to observe creativity in practice and action, the better. You may not consider yourself to be a 'naturally' creative or fun person, but that does not mean that your lessons and activities cannot be creative, fun, meaningful and beneficial to learning. You may not intend to work with younger children, but a visit to a children's centre or nursery, will be an eye opening experience, as you observe what children can do independently and using their own initiative.

If undertaking a placement in an alternative setting, there should be many opportunities to be creative in your approach to learning and teaching. In 'fun', 'out-of-school', 'field trip' situations you can develop a range of strategies, activities, tasks, learning opportunities, generally beyond the confines of a specified curriculum which you will be able to bring back to the classroom. Carolyn took the opportunity to be creative, in the creative environment of an art gallery!

Case Study: Carolyn – Art Gallery

This placement linked directly to the following TDA (2008) QTS Standards:

Q30: Identify opportunities for learners to learn in out-of-school contexts

Q32: Identify opportunities for working with colleagues, sharing the development of effective practice with them

Q25a: Use a range of teaching strategies and resources

But I am sure I met many more during my time at the gallery. It turned out to be one of my most successful placements although it wasn't assessed by the University. The reason it was successful is that in those three weeks my views on what constitutes good practice in teaching were overturned. Teaching in an art gallery taught me that good pedagogy extends far beyond the walls of a classroom. DfES (2003) The Excellence and Enjoyment Strategy stated that children learn better when they are excited and engaged. I concur completely and believe that at the heart of good pedagogy is the drive to creatively engage children in subject matter and exploit cross-curricular links in a way that makes learning meaningful.

I have seen first hand that a sure-fire way to get children excited and engaged is to take them out of the traditional school setting and provide them with opportunities to see and experience the stimuli provided by alternative learning environments. I would recommend that every student teacher complete a placement in an alternative setting because it really does open your eyes to a whole host of learning possibilities within contexts that you may never have thought about before.

Now it's easier than ever to set up a placement like this, with websites such as http://teachingoutsidetheclassroom.com/ which is supported by Creative Partnerships, CapeUK, Learning outside the classroom manifesto, Museums, libraries and archives council (MLA) and the Training and Development Agency for Schools (TDA). This website allows students on initial teacher training to locate and set up placements in a plethora of non-school settings. I have high hopes that, like me, many student teachers will take the opportunity to teach in an alternative setting and boost future creativity in the teaching profession.

The companion website to this book also gives you ideas for alternative placements.

Case Study: Gemma – Gambia

Gemma, and her colleagues who undertook a placement in a school in the Gambia, was given the opportunity to be creative, and to share her knowledge, understanding and skills with the teachers in the school.

> One of the achievements from the placement was the creation of a 'Resource Room', where the children could go to be creative. The children had access to paper, pens, crayons and pencils and we encouraged them to be creative through art activities and to produce displays for their class-rooms. We also developed some drama based activities, including role play and hot seating, which the children had not done before.
>
> Teaching in the Gambia was the most amazing thing I have ever done. It helped me develop as a person and to appreciate what I have in life and how lucky I am. It also helped me develop as a teacher. I was able to share the strategies and techniques that I used, with the teachers in the school, and their lessons became more active and creative. The teachers also began to use different questioning techniques, and discussion, and started to encourage the children to be more involved in their learning.

Consider:

- Why was it useful for Gemma to share her knowledge, understanding and skills with the teachers in the school?
- How could she continue to share her knowledge, understanding and skills with teachers during a traditional placement?

Impact of being part of a team on professional development

As a teacher you will always be a member of a team. You will rely on others, they will rely on you. Sometimes this will be easy; you will work with colleagues with whom you share ideas, beliefs, opinions and these colleagues may become friends. Occasionally you may work with colleagues with whom you have little in common, other than the need to do the best for the children or students in your care. Professionally, you should expect to work with these colleagues as effectively as possible.

Throughout life there will be people with whom you have a rapport, a shared interest and similar opinions; as there will be people with whom you have little contact and diverse or opposing views. This will be magnified within the confines of a micro society such as a school or classroom. Issues that may be fairly inconsequential within a broader context can become all encompassing and stressful in a restricted area of work. Being aware of this before starting a placement, and bearing it in mind, could help to ensure that potentially difficult situations can be managed effectively.

Jennifer undertook a placement at a Farm for City Children in Wales.

Case Study: Jennifer – Farm

I enjoyed every single part of the experience, even the messy parts like cleaning up the stables and pig sties, I can honestly say I have never felt more involved or as much a part of a team on any other placement. All the staff were brilliant, cared and gave us advice as needed. We also got advice from the teachers from things like how to get thirty odd children along a country road safely to handling confrontation (fights, etc).

I was very fortunate to have gone with two very good friends and I was able to see a different side to them, as we don't usually get the chance to observe and share tips with each other. Not only did I see a change within the children's attitude towards work, but I saw a massive change in confidence with my friends. I am more confident in working with animals, and with the situations that are involved with this (hygiene rules and where children would stand safe distance away, etc). I am more confident in speaking to adults and asking for help when necessary.

I have learnt so many things from the placement. There have been many situations that I have learnt from. For example, one child needed the toilet but because she couldn't take off her waterproof clothing in time she had an accident. I took control of the situation and spoke to the teacher with discretion and the teacher said I handled the situation really well. Another situation was when a boy with Aspergers syndrome became violent, we found that the teachers had been trained for this situation and handled it tremendously.

Reflect on the following:

- Consider two situations where you have worked as a member of a team, one that was a difficult experience, one that was a positive experience.
- Consider your role within the team in each situation. Do you think that your personality, temperament, prior experiences, beliefs, opinions and values had an impact on the role you played?
- How do you think others perceived your role and contribution?
- Are there any lessons that you can learn from positive situations that could be used in potentially difficult ones? Ask your friends and colleagues to comment, but don't be offended if they have suggestions to make!

Impact of placements on personal development

Personal traits such as confidence, reliability, dependability, sense of humour, empathy, sympathy, determination, endurance, willingness to listen, honesty, open mindedness, adaptability, flexibility, enthusiasm, commitment and dedication, will all be tested during any placement that you may undertake. These are significant elements in being a responsible, caring and motivated person, as much as being an effective professional. It may be easier to chart and record professional development against standards and targets, but personal development should not be overlooked and should be given due credit.

There are so many possibilities in terms of personal and professional development gained during placements, and the following are examples of these, to which you will be able to add numerous of your own.

Outdoor education centre

I was given full training up to Activity Instructor Position, a uniform and accommodation. I took sessions, planned a rota, undertook risk assessments and worked as part of a team. I really valued seeing a more practical side of education, being given responsibilities and being able to work with children and teachers in a completely different situation, (UG student).

Education centre (for excluded pupils)

The children had very challenging behaviour that could change at any time, which meant being very careful with what you said and using varied behaviour management strategies. I learnt so much about behaviour management and I believe this will really help my confidence when teaching. I feel that the placement was so useful that it's a shame others can't experience it, (UG student).

SureStart Children's Centre

I really valued the freedom to plan and teach my own creative activities linked to the Early Years Foundation Stage and art/creative development and to show I could be an innovative practitioner. It was good to be able to observe and work with children learning in a relaxed, friendly environment, through play, and researching and implementing elements of Reggio Emilia philosophy. I gained a greater insight into the Early Years, which will be useful for future experiences, (UG student).

Museum and art gallery

I worked with primary and secondary pupils on school trips and a half-term activity week. I also planned and taught a lesson for home schooled children, and helped the Education Officer with ongoing family learning projects. The experience gave me a great insight into what is required of a class teacher in preparation for a school trip to gain the best experience for the children. I was able to work with older pupils and a range of professionals, and to develop my adaptability to different situations, (UG student).

Learning support unit

I supported pupils with special educational needs in lessons and extra support sessions. It was useful to work with pupils and find out more about their needs and how to support them. It has increased my knowledge, understanding and confidence when working with pupils with SEN, which will be useful in mainstream teaching, (UG student).

Children's centre

In my previous placements in the classroom, lessons tended to be very structured, with very clear objectives and were very subject based. However, during the alternative placement there were different opportunities and learning experiences. Constructing displays with the children, in a less formal, fun and exciting way, created opportunities for cross curricular learning for the children, due to the broad topics taught. The whole idea of the centre was to give the children the opportunity to learn, but to provide an experience that was different from school based learning. I will definitely use approaches like these in my teaching in the future, to try and promote educational but fun learning experiences for all children. Everything that I have learnt from this placement I will use to help my teaching in the future, (UG student).

Impact of 'being a learner' on academic development

Learning is a life long process and the joy of being able to continue to learn throughout our lives is one we can relish. As teachers we are expected to teach, to educate and to inform others, but in this process we are constantly learning ourselves, from others, from situations and interactions. We encourage others to reflect, review, evaluate and analyse, to become active learners, advice that we would be wise to follow!

Case Study: David – Japan

For most of my placement in a Japanese Elementary School I assisted class teachers during lessons, although at times, to the amusement of the children, I would also join in as a learner. For example, when the second grade class which I spent most of my time in were beginning to learn 'shodo' (Japanese calligraphy), I would sit at a desk and learn it too. At all the junior and senior high schools I visited I gave a brief talk on English culture in several English classes. There would also be a question and answer section

Case Study—Cont'd

with the students for their speaking and listening skills. Students would record my answers and I would look at them after the lesson with the English teacher and provide some simple feedback. At the university lectures I attended I was there as a student so my role there was much the same as if I was attending a lecture in England. The exception being that I was often asked to explain things in more detail to the Japanese students by the professor.

The children at the elementary school seemed to be given enormous responsibility for themselves as well as others. The sense of community was evident at many different levels of the school, from class, to year group, to the whole school. One of my fondest memories is of the children lining up at the end of everyday in the playground, before they bowed in unison with the teachers and thanked them for the day's learning. The children then walked home in neighbourhood groups led by the oldest children. At first it all seemed alien to me but after returning to England I realised how important such small formalities were in establishing a sense of community for all involved.

Another common occurrence I witnessed through elementary schools to senior high was cleaning time. This happened for fifteen minutes after every lunch time. It involved the children and teachers cleaning the whole school. Classical music would be played through the loud speakers and children would spread around the school, sweeping floors, wiping desks, trimming bushes, weeding etc. . . . One teacher admitted it may not be the most effective method but it gave the children the responsibility of maintaining their school premises. I asked how everyone knew what to do, as the first few times I witnessed it seemed to work like clock work. I found out that each class was divided into smaller groups who followed a cleaning rota.

The most rewarding part of my time at the elementary school in Japan was similar to that of all of my previous placements, when the children take to you and accept you. This was something that usually came quite naturally when I had been on placement before and I'm happy to say it was the same in Japan, although the language barrier did mean that communication was much more 'fun'. It also reinforced the reason why I wanted to be a teacher and made me realise that the feeling and motivation I have experienced in England was not just in relation to England but anywhere when given the chance.

I believe that the placement gave me a real appreciation of the social skills children can develop, if encouraged to do so, in an appropriate and responsive manner. It made me question the incessant intervention that teachers can feel compelled to make in England. This is clearly something culturally bound and I am not suggesting that one system is superior to the other. However, when experiencing both, it made me able to recognise similarities, differences and basic realities of each system. This critical reflection was only enabled from the opportunity to step outside of my own culture and in doing so the constraints that come with it.

Case Study—Cont'd

> I began not knowing what to expect, and concluded the experience not knowing where to start to reflect, but without a doubt it has had a very positive influence on all aspects of my development and my role as a teacher. Experiencing the Japanese school system made me begin to appreciate other aspects of schooling that are just as, if not more, important than the academic side of school. For example, after school clubs played a very important part in all of the children's lives and lunchtimes were a class event, in the classroom, with the class teacher. Lunchtimes were when I got to know the children in my class best. I intend to take parts of the good practice I saw in Japan into my own classroom in England.

Part of being an effective teacher is to ensure that your knowledge and understanding is up to date, and that your academic development and expertise continues to grow. With this in mind, consider the following:

- Are there new skills, knowledge and understanding you would like to develop?
- How could you actively pursue the development of these?
- Are there language classes you could attend (possibly with Exchange students)?
- Are there extra curricular clubs you could become involved in, to enhance your skills, alongside the children's?
- Do you have a particular area/subject which concerns you – Art? Music? Science? Research this on the internet, read books, journals and articles. Discuss this with peers, colleagues and tutors. Keep a record of what you have done and the impact this has had.

Impact of subject knowledge and expertise on academic development

A key element of becoming an effective teacher is having a secure subject knowledge and understanding of the areas you will teach. Many teachers acknowledge that they feel more confident teaching certain areas/subjects, compared to others. Teachers and tutors will be able to advise relevant texts, journals, articles and internet sites, but being proactive and accessing support, guidance and expecting to have to 'work h' will help ensure that a 'block' does not have a detrimental impact on your personal and professional development.

Adam, a KS2/3 student undertook a placement at an international school in Spain, with primary and secondary aged students. He took every opportunity to increase his subject knowledge and expertise, knowing that this would have a positive impact on his academic and professional development, and future teaching career.

Case Study: Adam – Spain

The placement had a positive affect on my development academically and professionally, and enabled me to further meet some of the QTS standards. Professional development involves staying informed of new developments and technology within teaching, as well as learning new ideas and seeing new teaching styles, which can therefore improve subject knowledge and understanding which is essential in improving my own teaching. I was given the opportunity to work with many high attaining pupils, where I needed very secure subject knowledge and understanding because if I knew the subject well, I would be better equipped to teach the subject effectively.

The placement also gave me an opportunity to look at how the school taught ICT at Key Stage 2/3. Lesson observations allowed me to gather new ideas, teaching and behaviour management strategies. Supporting during lessons and collecting schemes of work used within the school provided me with the opportunity to learn more about lesson planning and gain homework ideas, which would be useful when teaching in England. This allowed me to add more variety and depth to my own teaching, while assisting pupils who were advancing quickly with their work. The placement allowed me to be selective and therefore, was sensitive to my personal development needs. I was able to choose lessons, and aspects of lessons, I felt would be most beneficial to my subject knowledge. Coupled with regular discussions, I was able to learn from teachers who had worked in an international environment for many years and were willing to share their knowledge and expertise.

The opportunity arose for me to teach Business Studies to year 13 pupils. This presented two potential issues. Firstly, Business Studies is a subject I had not taught previously and so had limited subject knowledge. Secondly, I had never taught a sixth form class. After discussion with the regular class teacher, and a look at the Business Studies National Curriculum, I was able to gain an idea of what I needed to focus on within the lesson. The class size was also very small which made overcoming the second issue a bit easier. With a good lesson planned, effective teaching activities, and a bit of confidence, I was able to deliver the lesson successfully, to a number of different groups, without any behaviour problems.

The school also held other regular meetings. The Department meetings I attended gave me an insight into the issues of teaching ICT in the school and the next steps the teachers were intending to take within their lessons specifically for each class. Another meeting I attended was a year 12 and 13 progress meeting. This involved all sixth form teachers getting together to discuss the current attainment and effort of each sixth form pupil. This was beneficial to me as it gave me an insight into the methods that the school was using to help and support those pupils who were struggling, and how the school dealt with the pupils whose behaviour has become a problem. This was something I had not witnessed during my placements in the England. This was possibly because not all schools have a sixth form and

> ## Case Study—Cont'd
>
> the ones that do have a larger number of pupils than at this school, but I felt it was a good idea, as pupils could be tracked personally and their educational needs catered for before their grades suffer too greatly.
>
> As you review your academic and professional progress, it would be useful to consider the following questions:
>
> - Could you undertake audits to get a baseline of your knowledge, understanding and skills in particular subjects/areas?
> - Are there particular subjects/areas that need to be developed and 'targeted'?
> - Are you able to set yourself some personal and professional targets?
> - Can you keep a record of any reading, research, practice you have gained in this area, which has supported your development? Can you demonstrate this in practice?

In placement evaluations the vast majority of students stated that they have gained considerably from the experiences they have undertaken, and noted the fundamental, significant and positive impact of these on their continued professional learning and development.

Jaz, who undertook a placement at a school in India stated:

> Art is a most specialist area and I was particularly interested in the differences between approaches to learning and teaching art. Balancing respect for colleagues' approaches to art, while sharing our approaches, helped develop my collaborative skills. The mural project we undertook gave me experience of planning, organising and managing a large-scale project. This encouraged critical reflection of my own practice and how I can further improve my implementation of art in the classroom.

An undergraduate student noted:

> Undertaking the international placement in a Montessori school for children with disabilities (in Ireland) has had an exceptionally positive effect on my professional development and future teaching career. I gained a significant amount of knowledge about a variety of disabilities including cerebral palsy, muscular dystrophy and epilepsy. I have interacted with and taught children with a range of disabilities; spoken to their teachers and parents/carers; and observed a number of therapy sessions such as physiotherapy, occupational therapy and speech therapy. These experiences gave me an insight into the support available beyond the classroom, and the way in which all practitioners need to work together to ensure children's specific needs are addressed.

The enthusiasm and exuberance of the students on return from their respective placements; and the value of the experiences they gained in terms of personal, academic and professional development and increased confidence, were significant and bode well for their teaching careers.

Key points

- Every placement you undertake will contribute to your development; personal, academic and professional.
- Taking time to review the placement and to consider what you have learned from it, will help to focus on your future development.
- Consider the impact that the placement has had on you as a person, as well as you as a teacher.
- Consider how your experiences have enhanced and contributed to your practice, educational beliefs and pedagogy.
- The placement may have been a life enhancing or even a life changing one; share this with others and inspire them to follow your lead.

Resources

www.britishcouncil.org/learning-tipd.htm

www.field-studies-council.org/professional/inservicetraining.aspx

www.tda.gov.uk/teachers/continuingprofessionaldevelopment.aspx

www.teachernet.gov.uk/professionaldevelopment/

www.teachers.tv/videos/common-core-of-skills-and-knowledge-personal-development-and-sharing-information/

www.teachers.tv/videos/professional-development/

Websites

Chapter 1 Why Go on Placement?

www.steinerwaldorf.org.uk
www.teachingoutsidetheclassroom.com

Chapter 3 Preparation is a Key to Success

Foreign and Commonwealth Office
www.fco.gov.uk/en/travel-and-living-abroad/travel-advice-by-country/

This site will also provide links to relevant Foreign Embassies and the London Diplomatic list:
www.fco.gov.uk/en/travel-and-living-abroad/travel-advice-by-country/
www.fco.gov.uk/resources/en/protocol/ldl-August2010/

The Department of Health website:
www.fco.gov.uk/travel/
www.locate.fco.gov.uk/locateportal/
www.nhs.uk/nhsengland/Healthcareabroad/pages/Healthcareabroad.aspx

Chapter 5 Look, Listen and Learn

Emotional intelligence
www.cipd.co.uk/subjects/lrnanddev/selfdev/emotintel.htm

Chapter 7 Overcoming the Challenges

Child Protection
www.kidscape.org.uk

National Society of Prevention of Cruelty to Children (NSPCC): 0800 800 5000
Bereavement
www.beaviour4learning.ac.uk
www.childbereavement.org.uk
www.crusebereavementcare.org.uk

www.rd4u.org.uk [for young people]
www.tda.gov.uk
www.teachernet.gov.uk
www.winstonswish.org.uk

Chapter 8 When Things Do Not Go to Plan

http://nationalstrategies.standards.dcsf.gov.uk/primary/primaryframework/
http://publications.education.gov.uk
http://tre.ngfl.gov.uk
www.bbc.co.uk/schools/
www.channel4learning.com/index.html
www.mape.org.uk/activities/index.htm
www.qcda.gov.uk
www.ttrb.ac.uk

Chapter 9 A Life-changing Experience?

www.britishcouncil.org/learning-tipd.htm
www.field-studies-council.org/professional/inservicetraining.aspx
www.tda.gov.uk/teachers/continuingprofessionaldevelopment.aspx
www.teachernet.gov.uk/professionaldevelopment/
www.teachers.tv/videos/common-core-of-skills-and-knowledge-personal-development-
    and-sharing-information/
www.teachers.tv/videos/professional-development/

Bibliography

Austin R. (2007) *Letting the Outside In: Developing Teaching and Learning Beyond the Early Years Classroom*. Stoke-on-Trent: Trentham

Bennett, L. (2007) *Travellers: The Gambia*. Peterborough: Thomas Cook Publishing

Black, P. et al. (2003) *Assessment for Learning: Putting it into Practice*. Berkshire: Open University Press

Bloomfields, P. et al. (2007) 'Creative Approaches to Staff Development: Global Education in ITE in the Gambia' in *Education 3–13*. 35:2, 117–131

Boye, B. (2007) Gambia News Community. Available at: *http://wow.gm/africa/gambia/abko/article/2007/10/17/quality-education-ps-on-working-conditions-of-teachers*

British Council (2008) *Erasmus Programmes*. Available at: *www.britishcouncil.org/erasmus*

Byram, M. (2004) *Routledge Encyclopaedia of Language Teaching and Learning*. London: Routledge

Clarke, S. (2006) *Targeting Assessment in the Primary Classroom: Strategies for Planning, Assessment Pupil Feedback and Target Setting*. London: Hodder Murray

Claxton, G. (2006) 'Thinking at the Edge: Developing Soft Creativity' in Cambridge Journal of Education 36:3, 351–362

Cohen, L.; Mannion, L.; Morrison, K. and Wyse, D. (2010) (5th Ed) *A Guide to Teaching Practice*. London: Routledge

Craig, I. (1991) (2nd Ed) *Managing the Primary Classroom*. Essex: Longman Group UK Ltd

Craig, P. (2006) 'The Key to Successful Behaviour Management is . . . you!' in *Education Review* 19:1, 65–70

Cullingford, C. (1989) *The Primary Teacher: The Role Of the Educator and the Purpose Of Primary Education*. London: Cassell Educational Limited

Dean, J. (2008) (4th Ed) *Organising Learning in the Primary School Classroom*. Surrey: Routledge

Department of State for Education – Republic of the Gambia (2006) *Grade 1 teacher's book*. Malaysia: Macmillan

DfES (2003) *The Excellence and Enjoyment Strategy*. London: Crown

DfES (2005) *KS2 Framework for languages*. London: Crown

DfES (2005) *Languages for All: Languages for Life*. London: Crown

DfES (2006) *Learning Outside the Classroom*. London: Crown

DfES (2007) *Statutory Framework for the Early Years Foundation Stage*. London: Crown

Drummond, M. J. (2004) *Assessing Children's Learning*. London: David Fulton Publishers.

Dunne, R. and Wragg, T. (1994) *Effective Teaching*. London: Routledge

Fisher (2007) (3rd Ed) *Starting from the Child*. Maidenhead: Open University Press

Gibbons, P. (2002) *Scaffolding language, scaffolding learning: Teaching second language learners in the mainstream classroom*. London: Greenwood Press

Goleman, D. (1995) *Emotional intelligence: why it can matter more than IQ*. New York: Bantam

Hayes D. (2003) *A student teacher's guide to Primary School Placement: learning to survive and prosper.* London: RoutledgeFalmer

Holly, M. L. (1989) *Writing to Grow. Keeping a personal-professional journal.* Portsmouth, New Hampshire: Heinemann

Jagne (2007) Gambia News Community. Available at: *http://wow.gm/africa/gambia/abko/article/2008/2/28/quality-education-is-fundamental-to-success-abuko-principle*

James, J. and Shields, Jr. (Eds) (1995) *Japanese Schooling: Patterns of Socialization, Equality and Political Control.* Pennsylvania: The Pennsylvania State University Press

Kerry, T. and Kerry, C. A. (1997) *'Differentiation: teacher's views of the usefulness of recommended strategies and helping more able pupils in primary and secondary classrooms in* Educational Studies, 23:3, 439–456

Klug, R. (2002) (4th Ed) *How to Keep a Spiritual Journal. A guide to journal keeping for inner growth and personal discovery.* Minneapolis: Augsburgin

Lee, S. et al. (1995) *'Teachers and Teaching: elementary schools in Japan and the United States'* in LeTendre, G and Rohlen, T (1996) (Ed) *Teaching and Learning in Japan.* New York: Cambridge University Press

Leonard, J. S. (1991) *Education Reform in Japan: A case of Immobilist Politics.* London: Routledge

Lightbrown and Spada, N. (1999) *How Languages are Learned.* Oxford: Open University Press

Macaro, E. (2001) *Learning Strategies in Foreign and Second Language Classrooms.* London: Continuum

Medwell, J. (2007) *Successful Teaching Placement: Primary and Early Years.* Exeter: Learning Matters

Mitchell, R. and Moyles, F. (2004) *Second Language learning Theories.* London: Arnold

Moon, J. (1999) *Learning Journals: A handbook for academics, students and professional development.* London: Kogan Page

Naumann L. P.; Vazire S.; Rentfrow P. J. and Gosling S. D. (2009) *Personality and Social Psychology Bulletin.* December 2010

O'Brien, T. and Guiney, D. (2001) *Differentiation in Teaching and Learning: Principles and Practice* London: Continuum

Pandey, S. (2004) *Teacher education researches in developing countries: a review of Indian studies* in Journal for Education for Teaching. Vol: 30, 206–223

Pandey, S. (2006) *'Para-teacher scheme and quality education for all in India: policy perspectives and challenges for school effectiveness'* in Journal of Education for Teaching. Vol: 32, 319–334

Pollard, A. (2000) (3rd Ed) *Reflective Teaching in the Primary school: a handbook for the classroom.* London: Continuum

Pollard, A. and Tann, S. (1997) (3rd Ed) *Reflective Teaching in the Primary School: A Handbook for the classroom.* London: Cassell

Rainer, T. (1978, 2004) *The New Diary. How to use a journal for self-guidance and extended creativity,* Los Angeles: J. P. Tarcher Inc

Sage, R. et al. (2006) *The Dial Project- Research Paper.* Leicester: University of Leicester

Smith, D. (2001) *The Spirit of the Foreign Language Classroom.* Nottingham: The Stapleford Centre

Smith, M. (1999, 2006), 'Keeping a learning journal', *the encyclopedia of informal education.* www.infed.org/research/keeping_a_journal.htm

TDA (2008) *Requirements and Standards for Initial Teacher Training*. London: DfES

Tomlin, A. (2008) *'Sssssound effects' Report* in the magazine from the Association of Teachers and Lecturers. January/February 2010, 9

Tooley, J. et al. (2007) *Private schools and the millennium development goal of universal primary education: a census and comparative study in Hyderadad, India* in Oxford Review of Education. Vol 33, 539–560

Watson, K. (2001) *Doing Comparative Education Research*. Oxford: Symposium Books

Wearmouth, J. et al. (2004) *Inclusion and Behaviour Management in Schools: Issues and Challenges* London: David Fulton Publishers

Yoneyama, S. (1999) *The Japanese High School: silence and resistance*. London: Routledge

Index